HEM

HEM
Dressing The Body
AND NOT
Addressing The Soul

OLIVIA YVE

XULON PRESS

Xulon Press
2301 Lucien Way #415
Maitland, FL 32751
407.339.4217
www.xulonpress.com

© 2019 by Olivia Yve

All rights reserved solely by the author. The author guarantees all contents are original and do not infringe upon the legal rights of any other person or work. No part of this book may be reproduced in any form without the permission of the author. The views expressed in this book are not necessarily those of the publisher.

Printed in the United States of America.

ISBN-13: 978-1-5456-7289-1

TABLE OF CONTENTS

Church Check 1

When You Peel an Onion, Tears Are Soon to Follow 15

Satan Himself 27

Birthday Party Surprise 39

Clouded Judgment 49

It's Hard to Say Goodbye 67

Lord, Deliver Her 79

CHURCH CHECK

A LONG, STRESSFUL NIGHT FOUND TIARA in a familiar situation. But she was not aware of just how unfamiliar this night would turn out to be.

The music lowered, the smoke cleared through the cracked window, and the car stopped. Parked outside the Radisson Down City Hotel, Tiara began to look around at the people and surroundings. She felt the strength of Satan himself gripping her thigh. "You're hurting me!" she begged as she looked into his red-tinted, soulless eyes.

"Good. I don't chase hoes. When I call, you pick up immediately," he said, tightening his grip.

"Ok." She began to cry.

"Don't mess up your face. Now listen…" He patted her on the head, not wanting her emotions to get in the way of her performance. He explained the importance of this client. "He's well-known; you've probably seen him or heard of his name…regardless, what's the rules?"

"No names and no phones," she whispered.

HEM

This was the trap in which Tiara found herself. She wanted God to just take her soul right then and there. She had done everything that Willie and Shy taught her about church. "God, I tried to abide by the rules." She pleaded in her heart for God to see her efforts and rescue her. It seemed like the "church check" that they had pounded in her head was irrelevant in this situation. *What did I miss?* She wished she could ask Willie how to use it in scenarios other than church. But Willie had her own issues with "church check" that had been pounded in her head since birth.

I should've stayed home, Wilhelmina Rose Morris thought to herself as her body ached from sitting on the hard pew bench. "Amen," she proclaimed, raising her hand and nodding in agreement with the speaker—not hearing a word he uttered, but just fitting in with the congregation. She sat in the large cathedral church with a mural of angels playing musical instruments painted on the ceilings, in the midst of her fellow choir members waiting for their turn to sing, all there to celebrate the forty-sixth Pastoral Anniversary of Pastor Andrew Douglas, a very popular pastor, retired sergeant of the army, and black activist for the city of Providence, Rhode Island. Yet Wilhelmina couldn't stop thinking that she should have been home celebrating with her family. It was her son, Will's, second birthday. *I shouldn't be here,* she thought as she shook her head in disagreement with her decision to attend the service. Interrupted by the rumble of applause, she stood with her choir and made her way to the front. Everyone in front of her was uniformed in white shirts, black bottoms, and a red tie or ribbon. She held out her hands, put a smile on her face, and directed the choir to rock to the music. Waving her hands, demanding the choir's every note high and low, she wondered what her baby was doing. Was her husband still upset with her choice to attend the service instead of staying with the family? Was she a bad mom, a bad wife? Was God even pleased with her at this moment?

"Are you serious? You're going to church when it's Will's birthday?" Adrian questioned but waved her off, not waiting for a response. "When is enough, enough?" He took little Will by the hand and stormed out the door. Being torn between church and family had been a battle Wilhelmina had fought within herself since the birth of her son. Born and raised in the church, she wore many hats: church administrator, choir directress, Young Women's Workers president, part of the women's department, church every Sunday, Bible study every Thursday, and the list went on and on and on. She wasn't prepared for the amount of time, energy, and selfless effort it took raising a child. Trying to please a baby, a husband, other family members, work, and church was taking a toll on her, but seeing the toll it was starting to take on her family frightened her. She fastened her shoe buckles around her ankle and wiped her tears before they hit the floor. "Church check," she sighed as she stood in front of the floor-length mirror. Nude stockings, closed-toed heels, mid-calf, loose-fitted black skirt, white blouse buttoned to the neck and tucked neatly, red ribbon tied around the collar, clear lip gloss, small, barely-noticeable earrings, and finally, hair up in a neat bun. Check list completed, she grabbed her keys and headed out the door.

"Excuse me, excuse me, excuse me." Interrupting Wilhelmina's flashback was her best friend, Shy, scooting down the aisle, making her way closer and closer. She plopped down next to Wilhelmina and whispered, "Girl, what is wrong with you? The choir tore the house down, Sister Vega fell out in the Spirit, Brother James is still in the corner getting it, and you looking uninterested." Wilhelmina looked at Shy with tears in her eyes and just shook her head. Shy and Wilhelmina had grown up together in the same church and every level of school through college. Shy knew her well enough to know something was really wrong. She reached over and rubbed

Wilhelmina's back. "We'll talk later," she whispered as she scooted back to her seat.

The congregation sang its final "amen," and Wilhelmina rushed her way through the crowd that was waiting to greet her. The sun that had been shining so bright when she entered service had now drifted and made room for the moon. It was close to little Will's bedtime and the end of his birthday, which she had spent mostly in church. She started her car and pulled out her phone. No missed call, no text, no picture of her baby, nothing. She wondered if she should call but then thought of the argument that might occur. Suddenly, a knock on her window startled her. "Oh, Lord," she sighed, rolling down her window.

"Good evening, Sis. Morris. God bless you. I see you're in a rush, but I wanted to come over and personally thank you and your choir for blessing us tonight."

"Oh, no problem, Pastor Douglas. It was a beautiful service."

He extended his hand. Reluctantly, she filled it with hers. "Well, you have a good night. And if you ever need anything, I mean anything at all from me, don't hesitate to ask," he said, motioning his thumb in circles around the back of her hand. She cringed at his crooked, slimy smile that revealed his gold-trimmed tooth. Wilhelmina snatched back her hand in disgust. Pastor Douglas was a good friend of her dad, but for some reason, he made her skin crawl.

Rolling her eyes and the window back up, she heard another knock. "Girl, what the heck. Why didn't you wait for me? Open the door. Let's talk," Shy demanded.

Church Check

"No, I can't. Gotta get home to spend whatever time is left for my babe's birthday."

"That's right, little Will's birthday. Is that why you're down?" She looked at Wilhelmina, waiting for an answer.

"All I can say right now, Shy, is when you get married and have a kid, quit everything that you are a part of in church—*everything*—'cause if you don't, there are gonna be problems. Take it from me. I gotta go." She rushed Shy out of the car.

"Ok, Willie, but call me later, please."

"Mommy!" Will happily screamed as his mommy opened the door.

"Hi, Mommy's birthday boy." She dropped her bag and kneeled down to squeeze her little man. "You have fun today?" she asked, wishing he could verbally express himself and tell every detail of his day that she had missed. The room got quiet, and she looked over to the sofa where Adrian sat. "Hey, babe," she said in his direction.

"Hey," he mumbled, without lifting his head from the video playing on his phone.

"Where did you guys go?" she asked, hoping her inquiries didn't spark a flame.

"To the playground, my mom's, and the toy store."

Willie took a deep breath. She wasn't good with expressing herself verbally, but she knew Adrian wanted and deserved to know how she was feeling. "Adrian, I'm sorry. I just feel so torn, so obligated, the pressure…"

"But where does family fit in?" he interrupted. Adrian was a man of few words—a simple, to-the-point, laid-back type of guy. He just spoke his mind and expected you to listen. Adrian grew up in church but did not have the attachment that Wilhelmina did. When he was fifteen years old, his love for God began to fade after the death of his best friend, who was shot by a bullet meant for someone else. He questioned God and was even angry with Him for years until he just stopped feeling for God or even thinking about Him altogether. He tried to convince himself God didn't exist. It wasn't until seventeen years later, when he met Wilhelmina in a coffee shop, that he even considered the thought of God.

It was a brisk fall morning in New England. Wilhelmina sat alone reading a book and sipping her caramel latte. Adrian walked in and stood in line to order. He scanned the place, and his eyes stopped when he saw this beautiful dark-skinned woman, her hair braided in a crown over her forehead, with a pearl necklace and earrings, a blue cardigan sweater, cream jeans, and tan mid-calf heeled boots, sitting alone. She looked up as she brought her cup to her lips and noticed him looking. *Awkward,* she thought as she rolled her eyes and continued reading.

A few moments later, "Whatchu reading?" There he stood, behind the chair across from where she sat. Tall, somewhat muscular, dark, smooth skin, besides a scar over his left eye and a perfectly-lined beard that formed around his lips.

"*God Is Mad about You.*" She closed the book to show him the cover.

"Hmmm, sounds interesting. You look almost done. You mind telling me what it's about?" he said, not really concerned with the book but the opportunity to talk to her.

With an uninterested face, she replied, "How about introducing yourself first?"

"My fault. I'm Adrian Morris." He extended his hand. "I saw you over here reading. It looks like it's a good book. Can you tell me what it's about?" he said with a sly smirk on his face. She shook her head at his slyness.

What could it hurt? she thought. Guys usually ran like a roach from Raid as soon as she mentioned God. *Hey, this would be no different.* "Well, my name is Wilhelmina Willard; the book is awesome. But wait, you don't have a job to get to, or maybe a family waiting on you at home?" she asked immediately, letting him know the must-haves and have-nots.

"Wow," he chuckled. "It's Saturday, so no, I'm not working today. And the only thing waiting for me at home is Rosco, my dog."

"Ok, ok, I'm just checking 'cause I didn't want you to be late." They laughed. Adrian pulled the chair out and sat across from this beautiful woman.

She began to tell him about the book. At first, he wasn't listening with his ears, only his eyes, as her lips moved. But he was distracted at the amount of times she said, "God loves…"

"I used to believe in God," he interrupted. He became serious. He began to tell the story of his best friend's death.

Wilhelmina saw the hurt in his eyes and thought to herself, *Wow, God, are You sending me someone to witness to? Lord, give me the words*. Finally, the words came to her. "I can relate to death, fear, anger, questions, all of that." She told the story of how her little brother drowned at a local beach during a family reunion. He was ten years old, and she was fourteen and couldn't save him. She had lived with regret, guilt, and anger for years. At that moment, a bond was formed. She explained that if it wasn't for God, she would have killed herself (as she had often thought of doing as a teen) or gone into a crazy house. Adrian had experienced those thoughts and even one attempt of suicide but never credited it to God keeping him.

Reminded of their first encounter and how she helped him through a lost time in his life, she walked over to the couch and sat next to Adrian. Quiet for a moment, she thought of how to express herself, how to spill her heart's secrets, how to allow her husband into a dark space that she had never revealed to anyone—not even to the doctors that had given her a diagnosis she wouldn't except. She looked over and saw little Will playing with his trains. With tears in her eyes, she turned to face Adrian. "Babe, look at me," she pleaded.

He sighed and put the phone down. Looking into her eyes, he saw her hurt. "Come here." He let out a deep breath, reached over, and pulled her into his chest. Wilhelmina collapsed in his arms and began to sob. She cried often but usually in secret—in the car, in the shower, in the laundry room—but never in front of her husband. She always carried herself as if she had everything under control—Superwoman, as she often referred to herself—when inside, she felt less than super, inadequate, and like she could never do anything right. She often wondered if she should've accepted the help from the doctor and why she struggled to this extreme with one child when people have multiple children and seem to do just fine. She felt as if she was in the worst reoccurring nightmare where she got second chances and always blew it or messed up even more than the day before. How could having a planned bundle of joy bring out such negative thoughts and feelings? Throughout the day, the majority of her thoughts were of how awful of a mom she was because she couldn't put a diaper on correctly, how they would be better off without her. Feeling so overwhelmed and zombie-like from sleepless nights, she often felt the urge to get away. In the middle of the night, she found herself roaming the aisles of the Super Walmart or just driving until she got lost, and it took her hours to find her way back home. According to her OBGYN, she had all the signs pointing to that diagnosis.

Worst of all, she felt like God wasn't listening, or listening but just letting her suffer. She was tired of the emotional rollercoaster of good moments immediately followed by sobbing moments due to frustration over anything and everything. Did He hear her silent tears she cried at night while her husband snored next to her? Did He hear the thousands of her "God, help me" whispers all day, every day? Was He not pleased with her listening to the Bible at work because she couldn't find time to read it at home? Was He not pleased with her presence in church five days of the week when she was mentally somewhere else?

She couldn't shake off the diagnosis...postpartum depression, they say. But she didn't want to claim it, believe it, accept it, or get help for it. How could she have depression when she was a child of God? She was a leader in the church. That was contradictory. How could she lead others to the joy of God when she was experiencing extreme sadness herself? *I can't be depressed,* she thought. *I can't have postpartum. How can I have a disorder from a blessing from God?* All her life, she had wanted a child.

Her doctor suggested therapy, but she couldn't possibly sit with a stranger and share the disturbing thoughts that ran through her mind, especially the worst one that turned her stomach—the thought that maybe praying for a child was a mistake. The hate that she felt for herself grew as the thoughts and emotions got stronger, and the rollercoaster never ended. That long red sofa in the therapist's office called her name. But she had to keep it together. What would people think if she lost it? Would they respect her or look up to her if she was flawed? How could she be over a women's group at church? Would her husband leave her? Would her son be taken away? What a disappointment she would be to her daddy.

Wilhelmina was raised in a two-family house, where she lived on the second floor with her mother, father, brother, and little sister. On the first floor lived her grandmother and grandfather, who was the pastor of the church they attended, River of Life Church. Basically born in the church, Wilhelmina quickly learned the do's and don'ts of how to act in and out of church. It wasn't your typical method of teaching a child right from wrong. She did learn that, but there were also other rules that followed, rules like: women must always wear skirts or dresses past the knee; they must always wear stockings; no open-toed shoes; arms cannot be shown; hair must be up and not hanging; women must sit straight and not be wild (another name for playful); and women must oblige whenever asked to assist or help with anything. The men had rules as well, but nothing as strict as the rules for the women. These rules weren't listed on a wall; they weren't written down in a handbook to study. They were just something you learned.

It was a strict household. Living right above the pastor and with the pastor's son, those church rules spilled into the house. Wilhelmina was always the odd one in school, but she got used to it. Her rules seemed normal to her and just the way things were. Besides, as

Church Check

a child of God, she was supposed to be the odd one amongst everyone else. It just didn't feel good to her. It wasn't until her brother died that she began to see the dysfunction of her family's ways. She watched her mom struggle to get out of bed for their morning prayers with her father telling her to "shake it off, we have church." She watched her mother struggle to care for her six-year-old sister, wipe her tears while ironing their clothes, dab foundation under her eyes to hide the evidence of sleepless nights. Wilhelmina watched as her mother sat in church like a statue with a painted smile and an occasional wave of the hand. She watched as everyone came and hugged her mother and said, "We're praying," yet neither the phone nor doorbell ever rang.

Her mother was never allowed to mourn, and neither was Wilhelmina. It was never talked about, and they never saw each other cry. This strange act continued for years until Willie turned eighteen. In college, she thought it would have been be easier to write a letter to her mom expressing herself. She shared how unfair it was that they couldn't mourn because it was considered out of control, and it was unfair to Johnny that they had acted like he had never existed. Wilhelmina invited her mother to meet her at the gravesite the following week on Johnny's birthday so they could visit him for the first time. There was no reply to the letter, and nothing was mentioned during their nightly phone conversations. Wilhelmina stood at the gravesite that had taken an hour to find. The small black-and-grey marbled tombstone was hidden underneath scrubs and weeds—never tended to. Her mother slowly walked up the path to where she stood, holding a dozen white roses. Then Wilhelmina released all the emotions she had swallowed for years. They wept in each other's arms, cleaned off his tombstone, and sat and recalled memories. They went their separate ways, and that day was never to be talked about again.

HEM

And now, Wilhelmina could feel herself drifting from herself, going back to the state of mind she was in after the death of her brother. Feeling an out-of-body experience, she slowly disconnected from herself.

"Babe, I need your help," she whispered as she tried to calm herself so she wouldn't catch the attention of little Will. "I need prayer. I'm slipping, babe, slipping. My mind...please, just pray."

Adrian squeezed her tight, really concerned with the way his wife was acting, having never seen her so emotional, fragile, and vulnerable. Married three years, she had always had it together. He remembered how she always held down the family in church, in prayer, taking their money and paying bills, keeping the house, cooking, making sure the baby was taken care of, and even bringing him back from his lost state of existence. "Dear God, I thank You for my wife, my beautiful wife You blessed me with. She is hurting right now, and she needs You like never before. Hear her, God. Comfort her. Give her direction and Your perfect peace like only You can. And help me; show me how to help as well." He leaned down and kissed the top of her head that was buried in his chest. "In Jesus's name, amen."

"Amen," she whispered.

"Amen!" little Will shouted while playing with his train set.

They burst out laughing. "Thank you, babe." Wilhelmina sat up, took a sigh of relief, feeling the weight lifted, and leaned in for a kiss. Though they had been in a season of silence and cold shoulders, it was nothing a genuine prayer from a spouse couldn't fix. There's nothing like knowing that even in a broken state, your man has your back. Feeling lighthearted, Wilhelmina got up. "Come on, Will, let's get ready for bath time."

"No babe, I got him. Go to bed early." Adrian felt inclined to give her a break, now seeing and feeling how stressed she had been.

"Are you sure? I mean, I feel bad. I hardly saw him today."

"I'm sure. Look at him, he's fine. Oh, I was thinking...what do you think of having a little birthday gathering Saturday for the little man? Just a little one here at the house."

"Saturday, ummm..." she stalled while she looked at the calendar on her phone. "*NOONDAY REVIVAL*," it read. She looked up at Adrian, looking eager to celebrate his son. "Ok, let's do it."

"Alright. I got the baby tonight, and you'll handle all the details for the party," he laughed.

She shook her head and walked away. "Of course." Flopping on the bed she sighed, "Revival."

WHEN YOU PEEL AN ONION, TEARS ARE SOON TO FOLLOW

BUZZ, BUZZ, BUZZ...A CELL PHONE vibrated on the dresser. Shy ran to the phone, as she had been waiting for Wilhelmina's call. "Private," she said as she looked at the screen, suspicious of who could be on the other end. "Hello?"

"Hello, Shyanne, how are you?" A deep voice questioned.

Unfamiliar with the voice, Shy responded, "I'm good. Who is this, please?"

"Michael." With her mouth wide open, she couldn't believe he would call after all this time. "Um, hello. Are you there?" he wondered by the silence.

"Yes, I'm here. Just wasn't expecting to hear from you again."

Michael and Shyanne dated for about a year and a half, and the last time they had spoken was over seven months ago. The relationship was always rocky, with Shyanne devoted to her daycare business, her responsibilities in church, and community outreach, and Michael always between jobs and only going to church for funerals and Easter. All her life, Shyanne was drawn to bad boys. Michael was known to be a womanizer, dependent on women for places to live, and a drug dealer, yet his charm, intelligence, and good looks invited her in.

They had met in Down City Mall when a little girl who used to attend Shy's daycare ran over and hugged her. "Ms. Steel!"

"Hi, sweetie, how are you?" After small talk with the now-kindergartener, Shy stood up to greet the gentleman holding her little hand. He stood about six feet tall with a caramel complexion, shoulder-length dreadlocks that could use tightening up at the roots, a baggy t-shirt, jeans, and Timberlands. "Hi, I don't think I've ever met you. I'm the director of the daycare she used to attend."

The man removed the toothpick from his mouth. "Hi, Ms. Shyanne. I'm Cassie's dad, Mike. Nice to meet you." After a short introduction, he asked if Shy could help him pick out some school clothes, as it was his year to do school shopping. They walked, talked, shopped, and ate. Standing at her car, Shy gave Cassie a goodbye hug. Mike leaned in and gave Shy a hug and a light kiss on her cheek. She looked at him with a smirk, not rejecting the embrace. Michael was thirty-three years old, only two years older than Shy. She felt some kind of connection but not as strong as he apparently felt. "Can I call you sometime?" he asked.

Shy had promised herself to stay away from the bad boys, but she couldn't resist. She had tried the good church boy, youth minister kind but was just not attracted to them. Her profession, demeanor, and religion were conflicts of interest to her type in men. She always had this desire to save the world and tried one relationship at a time with no success—they always seemed to do more damage than good. She had to peel the onion and see what was on the inside.

When You Peel An Onion, Tears Are Soon To Follow

"Who am I to judge?" was the motto she used to convince herself it was ok to be unequally yoked while dating.

They lived in a small city where it seemed that everyone had slept with everyone or knew everyone or knew somebody who knew everyone. Shy called her girl Willie. "Hey, do you know a guy named Michael Jenkins? They just call him Mike, I guess." She began to describe his features and demeanor.

"He doesn't sound familiar. Did you check Facebook?"

"Yes, but he doesn't have any posts since 2016, and it's just a picture of his daughter."

"Hold on, let me ask Adrian, 'cause you know, he's like the mayor—he knows everybody." They laughed. Returning to the phone, Willie explained, "Girl, girl, girl, you better run. He said he went to school with his sisters, but around, he's known to be like a pimp type—treats women like crap. Basically no good for you."

"Really? Pimp type? That's not what I got out of our conversations and his actions." Shy defended the guy she barely knew.

"Shy, I know you. Please leave that man alone."

Shy laughed. "I'm just checking him out; no one said we were dating."

Shy and Mike talked daily, got to know each other, and began to date. After many attempts to keep herself "saved," she failed and gave in to temptation. She repeated the mental cycle of devoting to keep herself sexually pure, then have sex, feel miserable after, repent, and start over again. This mental turmoil spilled into their relationship. She tried to get Mike to understand her dilemma. This was foreign to him, but he always told women whatever they wanted to hear. So he would agree to no sex during the day and rubbed and kissed on her until she gave in at night.

Mike was an unbeliever, unspiritual, and unreligious, so he couldn't understand the point of celibacy. He was raised in a home full of women—his grandmother, mother, and four sisters. He and his siblings lived in his grandmother's home while his mom struggled to get herself together. She was a prostitute and addicted to drugs. He often watched his mother get beaten by different men. Every week, he was introduced to a new uncle who would later blacken his mom's eyes and occasionally hand him five or ten dollars. Mike had no real relationship with his mother; he fell numb to the abuse she received and the sickness with which she struggled.

He didn't meet his father, a well-known drug dealer, until he was seventeen years old, and that was by chance. Mike, a high school dropout looking for fast money, was introduced to Joseph "Jo-Money" Taylor. After some months of Mike slinging for him, Jo-Money told Mike of their relation. "You can either get mad, or let's make this a family business and make this money," Jo-Money said, as if he was offering Mike the best gift a father could.

Emotionless and hooked to that fast dough, Mike responded, "Man, I'm 'bout this money." He brushed it off. Through the years, Jo-Money was locked up, and Mike held it down. Popularity, money, and nice cars brought along women, which, in turn, brought along several children who were close in age with two the same age. Mike had no respect for women. MOB, "money over bitches," was his motto. As he got older, Mike slowed down from the drug game and picked up some other activities in his late-twenties—activities he tried to keep secret while in a relationship with Shy.

WHEN YOU PEEL AN ONION, TEARS ARE SOON TO FOLLOW

After one year and five months of a vicious cycle of arguing, ignoring phone calls, females calling his phone, disappearing acts, make-up sex, and repentance, the relationship ended abruptly on Glendale Road. Driving down the road, arguing as usual, Shyanne noticed police lights in the rearview mirror. "What the heck?" she said as she pulled over.

"What's up?" Mike turned in his seat, nervous at what he saw. "Damn, girl, why you pull over?"

"What?" she questioned.

In the middle of the newly-erupted argument, the officer knocked on the window. "License, registration, and insurance, please." He bent over, looking suspiciously at Mike on the passenger side. "Sir, can I see your ID?"

Mike passed his ID along. The officer returned to his car to check them out. "Damn it!" Mike yelled. He punched the dashboard. "I'm screwed."

"What the heck is going on, Mike? What's wrong with you?"

"I'm dirty right now," he said ashamedly, "and probably got a warrant for something else."

"What? You know how I feel about that. And this is why... oh, my God!"

"Can you hold it for me? You'll get a slap on the wrist."

Shy turned to see if he was serious. How could he ask her to risk her life, her business?

Before she could answer, the officer was at Mike's door. "Sir, I'm going to need you to come with me. Were you aware that you have a warrant?" Mike argued with the officer while he was handcuffed and searched. Shy watched in shock as from Mike's jean pocket, the officer pulled a big zip-locked bag full of weed and a smaller bag with white powder.

"Oh, my God," she whispered. She began to pray that God would get her out of this mess that she had gotten herself into. A second police car pulled up and assisted the first officer in searching a now-irritated and argumentative Mike. "Oh, Lord!" she cried, praying harder. Not having the words, she could only repeat, "Jesus. Jesus. Jesus."

The second officer knocked on her window. She rolled the window down, and he returned her license, insurance, and registration. "Ma'am, how do you know this gentleman?"

"He's my boyfriend," she said in shame.

"You look like a nice young lady—no records, warrants, or anything. I don't know if you know what this man is into, but I suggest you stay away from him." He gave her a ticket for running the stop sign, which caused her to be pulled over anyway, and told her she could go.

"Shy, call my mom!" Mike shouted with his head pressed against the hood of the car. Shy pulled off with a mixture of emotions—disgust, anger, disbelief, and fright—but most of all, she was mad at herself. How could she have been so blind? She kept replaying the words of the second officer. She wondered what kinds of things Mike was into. She knew of his smoking weed here and there, but not enough to carry big bags. *And what was the white stuff?* she wondered. All she knew was that she never wanted to see or hear from Mike again. And she vowed not to...until now.

"What do you want, Michael?"

"Damn, girl, I haven't talked to you in forever, and this is the warm welcome I get? I missed you."

Silent on the other end, Shy shook her head and talked herself into not giving into his charm. "Mike, I really can't talk to you. It's not going to work. I'm sorry it had to end this way, but it has ended."

He interrupted her. "I never thought you would leave me cold though, Shy. You didn't even let my family know. I begged you to call my momma. You didn't even go and check on Cassie. That's foul."

She shook her head even harder, refusing to fall for the blame game. "Nope, it's not gonna work. Mike, I have to go. You didn't care about my business...could've got me arrested for your foolishness. I'm good. I pray for you."

"Bitch, keep your prayers...acting all holier-than-thou. 'Cause I know the real you."

Shocked at his disrespect toward her, Shy disconnected the phone. It took seven months to get back to normal emotionally. But here she was, back to disgust and anger, upset with herself that she hadn't hung up the phone the moment she heard his voice.

Shy immediately called her best friend, Willie.

"Hey, Shy, can I call you in the morning? Adrian is taking care of Will so I can go to bed early. I'm about to be knocked out."

Disappointed but knowing how rare an early night was for Willie, Shy said, "No, yeah, girl, get your rest; we'll talk tomorrow after work." She couldn't share her relationship life with anyone else. Wilhelmina was the only one who understood Shy's heart and relationship choices and still didn't judge. Sitting in her room in silence, Shy needed to get out of her own head. Usually, she would defeat boredom and crazy, selfish thoughts by staying active in church, working with the youth, and mentoring a teenage girl she had met at a local community center. But at this time of night, none of those were available. Shy turned on her phone's Bible app, selected "Audio," and listened to scriptures until she drifted off to sleep.

The next day, Shyanne sat in the office of her daycare, God's Child Care, for the majority of the day. The day's task of reviewing applications was replaced with replaying the events of the night before. She fought the flashbacks of her conversation with Mike as she replayed his words over and over, wishing she could change her response. She was disappointed in herself for repeating the cycle of dating bad boys. She wondered what it would take for her to run the other way when a thug approached her. *Knock, knock.* "Come in."

"Hi, Miss Shyanne, we're about to close the day," one of the teachers, Miss Dee, said. "Did you want to come out and join us in our song?" She noticed Shyanne wasn't her chipper self, full of excitement and interactive with the children as normal.

"Oh wow, it's that time already? Yes, I'll be right out."

When You Peel An Onion, Tears Are Soon To Follow

"Miss Steel!" the children screamed. Fueled by their love and excitement, Shy perked up and joined in their circle as they sang the dismissal song.

"Thank you, God, for another day. We learned, we danced, we ate, we played. You're the reason the sun shines; I'm so glad that You are mine. Thank you, God, for my friends; can't wait to see them again."

They all applauded, and the kids ran to their cubbies to collect their things. The school doorbell rang. It was Tiara Oakley, a high school girl that Shyanne had taken under her wing to mentor and help when she needed. Shy had been mentoring her for about five months. Tiara came from a rough part of the city. She lived with her mom, who was fifteen years older than her and was always asleep, drinking, or partying. "Hey, Tiara, I thought we were meeting a little later. Is everything ok?" Shy asked.

Tiara began to shake, and tears fell down her face. They walked into the office, and Shy closed the door behind her. "Come here," she said as she pulled Tiara in for a hug. "What's wrong?"

"He's back."

"Who's back?"

Tiara looked Shy in the eyes. "*He* is back." She emphasized "he," referring to an older guy who had been stalking her and trying to get her to trick for him until he was picked up a few months ago.

"Oh, him. He contacted you?"

"Yes! My phone rang, and it was him. He asked if I missed him and if I was ready for some more."

Shy wondered why this man would ask Tiara if she wanted more. She realized Tiara's stories were starting to conflict, and some parts were missing. "Tiara, I am here for you, you know that, but if you want me to help you, you have to be truthful. Why would he ask if you missed him? Did you have some kind of relationship with him already?"

Tiara was hesitant at first. "*What?!* No, no, absolutely not. He's old, like my mother's age. Nah, nah, hell nah."

"Ok, ok, I'm just asking." Shy was suspicious of Tiara's reaction. She knew she needed to tread lightly in helping her, or Tiara would shut her out. "On another note, what are you wearing?" Shy questioned Tiara, scanning her from head to toe.

The curvy teen's body displayed a white wife beater with a knot tied in the back, allowing her belly to peak through, short cut-off denim shorts, and a plaid flannel shirt tied around her waist. Tiara looked down at herself. "What? I'm covered with this shirt around my butt." She defended her wardrobe option.

Shy gave her a look of shame. "Tiara, you know better. Have you gone over your check list? It'll help you learn what to wear and how to carry yourself as God's daughter." She pulled out an extra list for Tiara to review.

They locked up the daycare and headed to church. It was Monday, when the youth of River of Life Church met weekly to socialize.

When You Peel An Onion, Tears Are Soon To Follow

"Alright, everyone. Everyone! Have a seat and let's get started." Shy opened up with prayer, and they all sat in the chairs formed in a circle. Each teen recited a scripture that helped them when they were going through problems. Tiara was fairly new to the group and was insecure with her lack of Bible verses and knowledge of anything spiritual. She felt as if she was the bad girl in the group. "Tiara, did you do the assignment? Do you have a scripture?" Shy asked, hoping Tiara would've used the Bible she had given her.

"No," Tiara said with a little attitude. Shy gave her a pass, as Tiara was new to the group, and she was in her feelings about her situation.

"Well, I think any of the scriptures mentioned today would be great encouragement for any situation you may go through." She winked at Tiara.

Tiara's cell phone began to ring. She ignored it and placed it on vibrate. The more she ignored it, the more it buzzed. Shyanne could see Tiara was getting more and more anxious every time she looked at the caller ID. Tiara caught Shy's eye and nodded her head, confirming it was him. "Ok, everyone. Thank you for doing your assignment. Thank you for opening up about what you're going through."

Shyanne looked at the agenda and cringed at the next topic to discuss. She knew it was mainly for Tiara, as she was the newest member. "Well guys, before we dismiss for pizza, I have to make an important announcement." She sighed. "Girls, this is just a reminder, but you know the dress attire for church. Church check before leaving the house. Stockings, skirt length—please, mid-calf at least—loose blouse buttoned all the way, hair nicely put up, and finally, no need for makeup. Maybe gloss." She tried to talk over the grumbles and moans. "I know, I know. But let's be obedient.

I'm going to ask Sis. Mills to close us out and pray over the food. I'll send a text with next week's assignment." After an uplifting prayer, the teens all shouted, "Amen," and ran for the pizza.

SATAN HIMSELF

PARKED IN FRONT OF TIARA'S HOUSE, SHY thought she'd try to get Tiara to open up again. "What did his texts say?"

Tiara stared out the passenger side window, thinking about what she had gotten herself into. Why would she mess up her life for a few dollars? "He just kept saying, 'Call me, call me.'" Tiara knew she could trust Shy. She had been there for Tiara more than her own mother, who was a stripper at night and slept most of the day. She would wake up long enough to order food or leave money on the table so Tiara could buy her own food. Tiara could never tell her mom what was going on with her. "You know better. It's my turn to do me" is what her mom always said whenever Tiara approached her with serious situations. Tiara had no one else to turn to until Shyanne Steel came into a community center that Tiara was a member of to teach a cooking class.

Tiara admired the way Shy talked, the way she dressed, and how she carried herself. She was so professional, but at the same time, she would play a game of one-on-one b-ball with the guys. Tiara would find herself studying Shy and mimicking her when she got home. They grew a connection, a playful big sister-little sister relationship. Both were the only child of their parents, so they appreciated their bond and called each other sisters. Still, no matter how close the connection or bond was, Tiara couldn't let it break through the wall she had built to protect her secrets. The only ones she could trust were the white pages that filled her pink leopard composition book she kept tucked deep in her underwear drawer. Pages can't talk, lie, exaggerate, or judge. You get what you get. Tiara told the pages the awful nightmares that occurred almost every night, except the nightmares were reality. She couldn't let her emotions and feelings of love toward Shyanne expose her. She already felt like her mom resented her for being born, so how would she feel, or would she feel at all? Would her secret affect her living situation? Would people hate her because her secret was not just her own, as it would affect others involved as well? There were too many unknowns.

"Are you sure?" Shy questioned how lightly Tiara took the continuous phone calls.

"Yeah. I'm fine." Tiara tried to ease Shy's concern.

"I know me and your mom have had issues, but have you told your mom? I can sit with you while you tell her, but you have to…" Shy was interrupted by Tiara's loud sigh.

"Shyanne, I'm fine. I appreciate you, but leave it alone. I gotta go." She jumped out of the car and ran up the stairs of her apartment, closing the door behind her before Shyanne could have the chance to react. Tiara knew once she was in her house, she was safe, assured that Shy wouldn't want another incident like the last one that had occurred when Shy tried to talk to Tiara's mom.

On another Monday, Tiara came to the community center with bruises on her arms and didn't return for a few days. Shyanne grew nervous and went by Tiara's house. She rang the bell a few times and then banged on the door. After several minutes, the door opened, revealing a woman wearing nothing but a stained white t-shirt, braless, with a cigarette between her fingers, long red nails, smeared red lipstick, and multicolored hair that ran down her back to her uncovered butt. "Hi, um, I'm Shyanne Steel from the community center. Is Tiara home? We haven't seen her in a while… just want to…"

"Just wanna what?" the lady abruptly interrupted.

Shy was shocked by her response and her attitude for Shy's concern. She thought of another approach. "I'm sorry, are you her mom?"

"Yes, I'm her mom, bitch. I'm her mom, so you ain't gotta come over here pretending to be concerned. Just turn yo' ass around with your business jacket on and get in your sporty car and go back to your white neighborhood." She flicked her cigarette in Shyanne's direction and slammed the door.

Tiara walked up the street and saw Shyanne's white two-door Mazda 6 convertible speed off. "I had to tell your fake ass sister off, coming to my god damn house," her mother argued. Tiara was embarrassed that Shy had to see her mother's condition at that moment, slightly hungover.

And now Tiara watched out of the peephole as Shyanne sped off again. She felt bad for not letting Shyanne in, but she had no choice. "Ma!" she screamed to see if her mom was home. Home alone as usual, while cold Chinese food sat on the table. *Buzz, buzz…*her heart began to race. "Hello?" she decided to get it over with. After several cuss words coming from the other end of the phone, she finally chimed in, "You promised me I could stop when I wanted.

I don't want to do it anymore," she begged. Falling on deaf ears, the conversation ended, and Tiara went into her room.

A while back, he had given her a white box to only be opened when the job required it. He had instructed her that this job was special. Buried underneath a pile of clothes in her closet was the white box. She opened it and pulled out a navy-blue spaghetti strapped mini dress, a white thong, and blue-and-pink flowered heels.

She pulled her mom's makeup case from under the bathroom sink. Staring face to face in the mirror, Tiara tried to steady her hands as she applied foundation, eyeliner, mascara, eye shadow, blush, and Mac Plumful lipstick as her mom had taught her. Lastly, she pulled from the white box a long brown wig with blond highlights that fell to the middle of her back. Annoyed with the discomfort of the thong, she slipped on the dress that barely reached her thigh. She sprayed perfume in her hands and rubbed it along her arms, legs, hair, and chest. *Buzz, buzz...*she stared at her phone as the call from Satan himself hounded her. "Hello," she whispered.

"Let's go; I'll be at the spot in fifteen minutes."

One last look in the mirror. She put on her long tan hooded trench coat, grabbed her clutch, and headed out the back door. Walking the dark streets of her neighborhood with which she was so familiar, tonight she was a stranger to her neighbors as they watched this woman with long brown hair and heels strut down the street. She grew anxious and tried to compose her fear as she approached the bus stop where she was to be picked up.

God, she thought, *I don't really know how to pray like the other kids at church. I don't even know what to say. I'm just really scared.* Startled by a loud horn, Tiara walked toward a 2001 black two-door

Acura TL with dark, tinted windows and music pounding. The window slowly descended, and a continuous cloud of smoke rushed to escape. "Get in," he commanded. Tiara got in the car and stared out the window as they drove to the special destination.

What the hell. If there was a God, would I be in this hell? Tiara questioned, convincing herself there was no one that could help her—not her mother, not Shyanne, and damn sure not a God she'd never seen.

The music lowered, the smoke cleared, and the car stopped. Parked outside the Radisson Down City Hotel, Tiara began to look around at the people and her surroundings. She felt the strength of Satan himself gripping her thigh. "You're hurting me!" she begged as she looked into his red-tinted, soulless eyes.

"Good. I don't chase bitches. When I call, you pick up immediately," he said, tightening his grip.

"Ok." Tiara began to cry.

"Don't mess up your face. Now listen…" He patted her on the head, not wanting her emotions to get in the way of her performance. He explained the importance of this client. "He's well-known. You've probably seen him or heard of his name…regardless, what are the rules?"

"No names and no phones," she whispered.

"Hand it over. Don't screw this up for me. It's his first time using me, and I told him I had someone special just for him—young and tight." He began to rub his hand up her dress. "He paid big money, so he's getting the full package tonight."

Tiara swung her head around to face him. Feeling a burst of bravery, she shouted, "What? Hell no! I'm not doing that." She folded her arms and leaned back in the seat.

He chuckled and clenched her leg tighter. "You will. You'll act like you love it, and if I find out you didn't…" Not needing to finish his statement, he reached under his seat and pressed the barrel of a black 9mm gun against her thigh.

"Ok," Tiara whispered, recognizing the seriousness of the situation and just how trapped she was in the game. He gave her a shot E and J and the hotel room key and said, "You have two hours. Be outside by 2:00 a.m."

She exited the car, removed a small perfume bottle from her purse, and sprayed herself to disguise the evidence of her smoky ride. Thoughts of running flooded her mind as she walked across the parking lot. Continuing to look over her shoulder, she wished the devil in the black car would drive off. *Should I run? Should I tell the hotel clerk? Should I call Shy?* All these questions she wondered as the hotel entrance grew closer and closer. Remembering her cell phone was held hostage, she dismissed calling anyone.

"After you, ma'am," the concierge said as he held the door open, examining her body, whose curves disguised her age.

She entered the lobby and looked around, admiring the elegance. How could something so elegant be less than a mile from her hood, where crack pipes lined the streets beside zombie bodies fighting over shopping carts filled with their possessions? This place was nothing like the dirty motels she was used to working in. A huge chandelier hung in the center of the lobby, and underneath sat a shiny black grand piano with a white man in all black tickling the ivories.

"Good evening, ma'am. May I help you with a room?" a perky receptionist rang out from the desk.

"No, thanks."

Tiara made her way to the elevator, catching the closing door. With each floor, her nerves grew. On the eighth floor, the door slid open, and she stepped out. Heart racing, she slowly walked down the long hall of death row. She stood at the last room on the right that read "8110." She pulled the door card from her purse and inserted it in the slot, slowly opening the door to a dimly lit room. Across the room, a figure sat motionless in a chair. "Close the door," his deep, raspy voice commanded. Tiara hesitated, distracted by the nagging thought to run. Ignoring the insistence of her conscience, she closed the door behind her. "Put the chain on the door," his demands continued. Tiara put the chain on the door, took a deep breath, and got into character. She turned to face him. Switching her hips as sexily as she knew how, she slowly switched toward the deep voice. He pulled the string on the lamp, standing tall beside his chair. She stopped suddenly in her tracks, in shock by the familiarity of his face.

In disgust Tiara, examined him from head to toe. The only noise that broke the silence was his heavy breathing. His large body rested in the white accent chair. Dye-stained hair aligned his lips and chin, and a black suite struggled to hug his large body, while a gold nugget ring squeezed every fat finger.

"Don't be shy, baby girl. You know what to do." He reached for her hand. Unable to move, Tiara stood in disbelief. *Not him,* she thought. The one thing in life that was supposed to be real and always true, her trust and love for God, was now clouded by the representative who sat before her. She slowly moved closer. He pulled her until she stood between his legs. He held her hand and began to motion his thumb in a circle around the back of her hand. Her body quivered in fear. She had crossed many lines in this business, but this was a first that she was absolutely not willing to cross. While his left hand was busy fondling her hands, his right moved slowly up her thigh.

Before he could grip any further, she snatched herself from his sweaty palms and pleaded for him to let her leave. She promised not to tell anyone, but he refused her persistent offer. He walked toward her, grabbed her by the hair, and pushed her to her knees. With eyes closed, wishing she could disappear, she heard the sounds of a belt unbuckling and a zipper unzipping. She watched his pants fall to his ankles. He forcefully pressed her face against his sweaty stomach, which covered most of his penis, and squeezing her cheek, he forced her mouth open. Refusing to comply, she yanked herself away, leaving only her wig in his grip. He struggled to regain his grip, tripping on his pants wrapped around his ankles.

Tiara ran to the door but was unable to unlatch the door chain fast enough. As he waddled in her direction, she ran to the bathroom and tried to lock herself in. He busted through the door and, with fire in his eyes, transformed into the devil himself.

"Please, please, don't!" she screamed. "Help!" She was able to burst out before he charged at her and grabbed her neck and smacked her across the face. He proceeded to choke her with one hand and pull on her dress with the other. Grabbing at his hands, she couldn't loosen his hold. Her fingers spread wide, desperate for anything to grab, but nothing answered the call of her reach.

Feeling consciousness beginning to evade her, with her last effort, Tiara clawed through his face, kicking and squirming. He struggled to keep his grip around her neck. He began to feel the burn from her sharp nails continuously digging into his face. The glasses that had once protected his eyes lay shattered on the blood-spotted tile floor. He grabbed his face in agony.

As she gasped for air, Tiara griped her throat, wondering if the struggle was over. Vision blurred and out of breath, he slowly walked toward Tiara, who grabbed the coffee pot that sat on the bathroom counter.

"Please," she began to sob. "I won't tell anyone. Just let me go." He continued to take steps forward, grunting in pain with every step. "Please," she begged one last time as he extended his arm and grabbed her dress. Tiara closed her eyes and, with all the might she had left, swung and broke the glass coffee pot across his head. He screamed in agony, grabbed his head, and fell to his knees. With nothing but the coffee pot handle in her hands, Tiara attempted to slide by him. Almost out of the door, with one last effort, he grabbed her ankle. Refusing to let him overpower her, Tiara began to pound down on his head with the handle.

With every blow, she released a cry for the little girl who had been molested, the little girl who had been neglected at home while her mom stripped, the little girl who didn't have a daddy to protect her from predators and devils…one last blow for all the cries for help that had fallen on deaf ears.

His body collapsed on her feet. Tiara squirmed from his weighted body, grabbed her trench coat, ran out of the room, and bolted down the eight flights of stairs.

HEM

She steadied her pace as she entered the lobby, making no eye contact. With shoes in hand, she walked through the lobby and out the door, hoping no one would notice her. As soon as her bare feet touched the pavement, she began to run as fast as she could, avoiding the brightly lit streets. Her heart pounded in her chest; she feared running into her pimp. If the old fat man in the hotel room didn't kill her, he surely would.

She made it home, relieved her mom was not there. As she attempted to unlock the front door, she trembled, dropping to her knees every time a car passed by. Finally inserting the key, she turned the knob and busted in the door.

Tiara ran to her room, shut the door, fell on her bed covered with stuffed animals, and began to sob. "Oh, God!" she cried. "God, please!" Not knowing how to pray or what to say, she just pleaded for help.

She began to talk to God. "I know I'm no good, I know what I do is wrong, but I feel like I had no choice. You gave me no other choice!" She began to get angry, thinking of how she felt neglected by God Himself. "I started going to church on Sundays, youth group on Thursdays, and I even dressed right. I borrowed Shy's skirt, shirt, and stockings. She even checked and made sure I looked right." She sat up in her bed. "What else do You want from me?" she whispered.

Tiara paced the floor, wondering if she should call the cops, if the fat man was alive or dead, and if the pimp would search for her if she wasn't outside the hotel at two o'clock. "Shy!" she realized she could go to Shy's house, and Shy would help her figure it out. "Damn it, my phone!" she remembered the devil himself took her phone. The time on the cable box read "12:36." Tiara threw on some gray sweat pants, a hoodie, and black air force ones and headed out the door. She ran back in to grab her nightmare keeper, her pink leopard journal.

"1:02 a.m.," the clock read on Shy's cell phone. Struggling to fall asleep, she scrolled through the selection of shoes on sale at Nordstrom. She hadn't been able to sleep for days, wondering why Mike had been on her mind. She fought back the urge to call him daily. *Yes, he seemed to be troubled, but shouldn't we as Christians care and have compassion for those who are lost?* she thought. Yes, there were a lot of bad days, but she remembered all the deep conversations and even intimate moments they had.

A loud banging on her back door interrupted her reminiscing. "Who the hell is that?" She said as she jumped up. She grabbed her robe and the baseball bat under her bed and wondered if it was Mike. She maneuvered through the dark hall, then she tiptoed through the kitchen to the back door. She peeked through the blinds and saw a hooded figure standing under the dim light. "Who's that?" she yelled in her toughest voice as she gripped the bat, ready to swing at any moment.

"It's me, Tiara!" Tiara lifted her head and revealed the pain that had taken over her face. Shy quickly turned the lock and unhooked the chains that were bolting her door shut. She snatched the door open. Tiara fell in the door and collapsed into the arms of safety. The whirlwind of fear, survival, and shock had kept her moving and focused on getting to safety. All of her anguish bubbled up inside and exploded in the arms of Shy. They sat rocking on the kitchen floor. Shy stroked her hair and hummed until her sorrow quieted.

BIRTHDAY PARTY SURPRISE

IT WAS FRIDAY EVENING, A DAY BEFORE the birthday gathering for little Will. Wilhelmina sat on her sofa, phone in hand, stalling to hit the "send" button on the text she had drafted to inform everyone that she would not be attending the revival on Saturday. With her father now the pastor of River of Life Church, Wilhelmina felt more pressure than the other church members to attend every service, or she would be considered unsupportive. She didn't want to be viewed as a slacker because she chose to cancel to do something that wasn't church related. But this something was important: family.

Wilhelmina looked over at her precious baby sleeping on the sofa next to her. His innocent face gave her the strength she needed. "Send." She quickly sent the text. She leaned back and rubbed little Will's head, pleased with the courage she had to finally put her family first.

It was the morning of the party. Wilhelmina was running around decorating the house and yard. *Ring, ring*...her cell phone rang. It was her father. "Hi, Daddy."

"Hi, Willie. How are you? Getting ready for the party?" he asked.

"Yup, I'm glad it's going to be a nice day," she said, out of breath from placing chairs around the tables. "How are you, Daddy?"

"Well, Willie, I've been better. Got some sad news this morning. They found Pastor Andrew Douglas dead in a hotel bathroom."

Wilhelmina gasped. "No, Daddy. I'm so sorry." Pastor Douglas and her father had been friends. "How did he die?"

"Well, all the details are not out yet, but the way people and the news are talking, it was for church business."

"Hmmm. I'm not surprised," she mumbled.

"What's that supposed to mean?"

"Well, Daddy, Pastor Douglas has always creeped all the women out. He's a bit of a perv," she explained.

"Stop now; he's not here to defend himself or tell his side of the story. God have mercy. He just had that big anniversary service honoring him. I would hate for his reputation to be destroyed."

"His reputation?" Willie began to debate.

"That's enough, Willie. I'll stop by the party after service. I just wanted to tell you. Bye-bye."

"Bye, Daddy."

It was 2:00 p.m., and friends and family began to fill in the backyard, there to celebrate little Will, but all everyone could talk about was the death of Pastor Douglas. Next to the gifts table stood a group saying, "Girl, did you hear…" Over by the swing set, while pushing their kids on the swings, the moms said, "I heard he was with a prostitute. Here, look. They have a picture of the woman they are looking for on the news' Facebook page."

At this point, Willie couldn't help but join in. "Let me see." There in the picture was surveillance footage of a woman in a long wig and sunglasses running barefoot through the hotel lobby. "She's a tiny thing." The chatty women concluded the girl couldn't have done it.

Shyanne entered the backyard. "Oh, thank goodness. You have the cake?" Willie asked.

"Hey, yes, Tiara is getting it out the back seat. Why does it look so intense back here? Turn the music up. It's a kid's party."

"Oh, you haven't heard about Pastor Douglas?"

"No, what?"

"Go mingle—you'll get more info than I can give. Let me set up the cake."

"Oh, wait," Shy stopped Willie. "I wanted to tell you. I talked to Mike a long time this morning, and I invited him to the party, if that's ok. He said he can't stay long."

Wilhelmina rolled her eyes and walked away, waving her off. "Whatever."

Tiara placed the cake on the table. "Hey, Tiara." A teenager from the youth church group had approached her. "Did you hear about Pastor Douglas?" Tiara froze. "Are you ok?" the girl asked.

"Yes. I mean, no. What about him?" She stumbled, trying to find the right words.

"He is dead. Some prostitute beat him up in a hotel."

"How...how...h-h-how do you know it was a prostitute?"

"It was on the news. They showed a woman of interest goin' in the hotel and then running out with no shoes on. I knew he was a freak," the girl concluded as Shy turned up the music, drowning out all the chitter chatter. Everyone was finally starting to enjoy themselves. The food was served. Tiara began to set up for musical chairs when, out of the corner of her eye, she spotted a six-foot tall man with a caramel complexion and shoulder-length dreads. They caught each other's eyes, and both froze. Shy walked up to the man and hugged and kissed him. She waved over to Tiara. "Tiara, come here, I want you to meet Mike."

Tiara dropped the chair, paralyzed with fear. Shy and Mike walked over to meet her. "This is Mike." Shy introduced the two. Mike extended his hand. Tiara's chest rose up and down as her heart swelled with fear. "Are you ok, T?" Shy asked. "Don't be rude; shake his hand." Tiara placed her hand in his. With fire in his eyes, he murmured through his teeth, "Nice to *finally* meet you," as he squeezed her hand with a deadly grip.

Tiara snatched her hand from the grip of death. Her mind was racing, her heart pounding through her chest. *Do I run? Do I stand here and wait to be killed?* she thought. Shy was so proud to finally show everyone the fine face behind her stories; she was oblivious to the fear beaming from Tiara. Shy took Mike by the hand and introduced him to Willie. He appeased Shy for the moment, keeping one eye on Tiara, who had slowly begun to ease her way to the house.

She tried to avoid eye contact with the devil. She climbed the back stairs and grabbed the screen door handle.

"Tiara!" Shy yelled. Tiara froze and looked back in Shy's direction, now unable to avoid the piercing red eyes that beamed her way. "Can you grab Mike a beer on your way out, please? Thank you."

Tiara bolted through the door. She ran into the kitchen, not sure where to go or what she should do. If she revealed Mike, she would reveal herself and would go to jail for murder. *No, I can't let my secret out. What will everyone think?* she thought to herself as she paced the living room.

"Are you alright?" a deep voice asked her. Tiara jumped and turned in the direction of the voice. It was Adrian, Wilhelmina's husband. He had always been cool, laid back, and down to earth with the youth. "Hey Brother A, I'm...I'm..." Tiara couldn't describe how she was. Her mind was running too fast.

"I noticed you a little uneasy when Shy's friend came in." Tiara stared at him. She wanted to tell him everything but couldn't speak. "I don't care for him myself. He's not a good guy; I tried to tell Shy." He looked at Tiara's face and could tell she knew just how much of a bad guy Mike really was. "But you know he's not a good guy already, huh?" She shook her head, but her face said the opposite. "Hmmm. T, look at me." Adrian wanted her to know that she could trust him. "I know what this guy does out there. I know how he exploits and abuses women and girls. That's why I'm upset that he is here. My question is why are *you* upset that he is here? Talk to me, T. I'll protect you, for real," he pleaded.

The screen door slammed shut. Shy stood in the kitchen, looking at the two of them having an intense conversation. "What's going on in here? Tiara, why is it taking you so long to get Mike's beer?"

Tiara looked at Shy in disgust. *How could she be with someone like that? How can she protect me from the enemy when she is sleeping with him?* she thought.

"Tiara, I'm talking to you." Shy was confused as to Tiara's sudden change in attitude. Adrian was also disgusted. "You can't see it's your man that's the issue," he blurted out.

"Please, A, don't start," she said, brushing him off. "I already know you don't like him. That has nothing to do with me."

"Yeah, but you're not listening to why I don't like him. Or maybe T can tell you why *she* doesn't like him." He looked over at Tiara.

"What are you talking about? Tiara just met him today. She has no reason not to like him. Mike is a good guy…he made a mistake with selling drugs. He did his time, and that's that. Get over it."

Tiara boiled with anger toward Shy. She finally let it out, "Get over it?! Get over it?! Did you know all this time? Did you know?" Tears began to flow. "I'm sitting here, running from this nigga, running to you for safety, and you deliver me to him! How could you?" Out of the corner of her eye, Tiara saw a figure climbing the stairs. Through the screen, Mike stared at Tiara before he opened the door. Tiara couldn't take it anymore. "I'm out. You don't care. You want him to kill me."

Birthday Party Surprise

Tiara ran out the front door as Mike came through the back door. "Is everything ok in here?" he asked as he watched Tiara run down the street, keeping an eye on the direction she was going.

"Yeah, babe, everything is good. I don't know what's wrong with Tiara." Shy wrapped her arms around his waist.

Mike turned his attention to Adrian, who was staring intensely at him. "You good, bro?" Mike asked, sensing some kind of animosity.

"Nah," Adrian said, slowly shaking his head.

"Adrian, please don't. You know what, let's go outside, babe." Shy tried to avoid the drama. She turned and pulled Mikes hand. He snatched back.

"Nah, what's good, Adrian? You act like you have a problem with me."

"Homeboy, you're in my house. You weren't invited to my son's party. So yeah, I have a problem." Adrian turned to face Mike and continued. "I tell you what, you don't have to worry about me having a problem. You can go." Mike walked closer until the two were face to face.

Shy forced herself between them as they stared each other down. "Willie!" she screamed for her friend to come and control her husband. Wilhelmina ran into the house and pulled on Adrian's arm.

"Adrian! Adrian! Stop it." She tried to hold him back.

"Get out my house!" Adrian demand.

Mike pushed Shy to the floor. "Move, bitch. I don't need this shit. I know where you live, homeboy. I got you." Mike lifted his shirt, showing the handle of a silver revolver.

"You gonna threaten me in my house? You ain't the only one carrying, homeboy."

Mike chuckled as he slowly walked out of the door, keeping his eye on Adrian. He had no time for Adrian's drama; he wanted to catch up to Tiara. Shy sat on the floor in shock.

"What the heck is going on, Shy?" Wilhelmina cried.

"Yeah, Shy. Why would you bring that nigga to my son's party knowing what he does?" Adrian paced the floor, trying to cool off. Shy began to cry. She was embarrassed by the way Mike had treated her in front of everyone and confused at what Adrian was talking about.

Wilhelmina kneeled down to meet her. "Shy, what is he talking about?"

"I don't know! I really don't know," she cried out.

"She doesn't want to know," Adrian interrupted. "Ask her where Tiara went. That nigga did something to her. I know he did." Adrian waved her off. "I gotta get out of here and to *my son's* party. He stormed out of the back door to keep the party guests from being suspicious.

Wilhelmina tried to hold back. She wanted to ask Shy how she could have been so stupid and why she would bring Mike unannounced. She wanted to ask her why and when they reconnected in the first place. But pushing all her feelings aside, Wilhelmina helped Shy off the floor. "Go get yourself together in the bathroom. It's just another lesson learned."

Shy ran the water in the bathroom sink to disguise her sobs. She stared at herself in the mirror. "God, what am I missing?"

CLOUDED JUDGMENT

TIARA RAN UNTIL SHE COULDN'T RUN anymore. "God, help me," she sobbed as she ducked in an alley to catch her breath. She knew it was only a matter of time before she would be caught. Who could she run to, now that the one from whom she sought her refuge was sleeping with Satan? She stood there, feeling helpless and hopeless. She wondered where could she go and who would protect her. *No one. I have no one to turn to,* she concluded. Startled by a homeless man pushing a shopping cart along the side walk, Tiara ran to the only place she knew—home.

She ran up the porch and banged on the door. "Ma…Mommy!" she cried uncontrollably. The door never opened. She ran to the back door. "Mommy!" She banged on the door and the window, then tried to open the windows until she finally found one that was unlocked. She lifted it up and climbed in until she fell onto the kitchen floor.

She ran to her mom's room. "Ma?" She banged on the door. No answer. Her head spun. Overcome by a whirlwind of emotions, she thought to pray, but to whom? She wondered, *Where is God now? Where has He been all this time?*

"All this time living in hell, where were You, God?" She threw a plate against the wall. She paced back and forth in anger, then walked over to the liquor cabinet and grabbed a bottle of whiskey. She guzzled it until she couldn't take any more. "I did what I was supposed to! You didn't answer my prayers!" she yelled as she threw another plate and a few cups against the same wall. "Stockings, long-ass skirts, shirts buttoned to the neck, clean, neat bun, for what? For *what?!*"

Her legs weak from miles of running, she fell back into the fridge, knocking everything on top to the floor. She gasped for air, trying to catch her breath. Spinning among the mess she had made on the floor was a pill bottle with a mixture of Oxy and Perks. A calm came over her that she had never felt before. Tiara opened the pill bottle and dumped the pills in her palm. *Nobody cares...no one will miss me. This is hell on earth.* Tiara convinced herself that she was better off dead. *How did it all come to this? How did trying to do the right thing go so wrong? I followed the check list.*

Tiara sat in despair. Feeling she had no other course of action, no other moves in the game of life, she leaned her head back against the refrigerator and stared at the popcorn ceiling. Her mind, body, and soul were exhausted. She had been running all of her life, from house to shelter to house, from men, from her mom, and now she wanted to run from herself. "Why me?" she whispered. She closed her eyes and fell into a sleep that her body had been missing for three days.

Wilhelmina slowly approached Adrian while he recorded the kids dancing on the grass. "Are you ok?" she asked, rubbing his back.

"I'm good. But babe, I'm so worried about Tiara." He put the phone down and turned to Wilhelmina. "I told you Mike was a bad guy, but I didn't give details. I assumed Shy would heed my words. Mike pimps women out—especially young girls who look like women." He took a deep breath. "I really think he did something to Tiara."

Wilhelmina covered her mouth in shock. "Are you serious?" She shook her head, confused as to how her friend could miss signs of such perversion. "I just don't get it." She tried to find the words to defend her friend.

Adrian scrolled through his contacts. "I'm gonna call Chuck. I think he's working today. I'm gonna send him to her house—just to check on her. I just have a bad feeling."

Shy stood on the back porch, debating if she should stay or leave. She had too much on her mind and needed to assess the situation and her life. Wilhelmina waved for Shy to come to her. Not wanting to see or talk to Adrian, Shy declined and waved for Wilhelmina to come to the porch.

Wilhelmina stormed over. "Look, we need Tiara's address. We're sending a detective over to check on her."

"What? Why?" Shy was confused.

"Wake up, Shy. Your man is a pimp. We just want to make sure she's ok." Wilhelmina became agitated and disgusted by her friend's cluelessness. Adrian walked over and handed Shy the phone. "Please give him Tiara's address."

Still upset with Adrian, Shy snatched the phone from his hand. "Hello? The address is 265 Brenn Street. The doorbell doesn't work." She returned the phone and walked back into the house.

Tiara sat on the kitchen floor, the whisky pulling her deeper and deeper into sleep. Silence filled the house. Peace fell upon her face as dreams of being in happier places rocked her—dreams of laying on her grandpa's farm surrounded by little chicks tickling her with their colorful beaks. Suddenly the ground opened underneath her, and she fell onto a wagon full of hay being pulled by a faceless man with the body of a horse. Tiara looked up at the deep blue ocean of water that filled the sky as the creature pulled the wagon through an orchard. Colorful apples slowly fell from the sky, and she extended her arm to catch one. The apples popped like bubbles as she made contact with them. She smiled, fascinated as the apple bubbles burst against her nose. The apples dissolved, covering the sky with one huge pink cloud. The wagon suddenly tipped over, and Tiara fell onto the fluffy pink cloud. The puff accelerated. She tried to hold on but was unable to grip the cloud as it crumbled in her hand. The deep blue ocean sky then turned black. Lightening began to pierce the cloud. With each strike, a piece of the pink cloud burst into flames, then its ashes blew in the wind. Rumbles quickly turned to cracking. No longer amused by the dream-turned-nightmare, Tiara fought to hold on to the cloud that had dwindled to a size that could barely hold her. *Bang, bang, bang.* She looked up, and lightning bolts fell on her head with a final bang.

She gasped and woke up. *Bang, bang, bang.* There was pounding on the door as Tiara sat motionless on the floor. "It's him! It's him!" She whispered in a panic. She opened her palm and looked at the pills that filled her hand. She began to rationalize. "I'm dead anyway. He's going to kill me." She dumped the pills in her mouth and guzzled the remaining whiskey.

The banging ceased. Tiara closed her eyes, hoping to quicken the permanent sleep that awaited her. She longed to warp back into the deep blue sky, riding on her pink cloud through a thunder storm, anything other than being tortured and killed by Satan himself. Tiara wondered what would be waiting for her on the other side. *What will God look like? Will He even let me in?* "I tried, God." She gave one last plea for God to see that she did try. "I tried to learn scriptures. You know I tried to get my mom to buy me church clothes. I did. I tried." Tears fell down her face. *If only I could go back. When that shiny black car with rims and pounding music pulled alongside me, I would not have been impressed. And when the tinted window rolled down to reveal the devil disguised in smooth, caramel skin with long, winding snakes disguised as dreads hanging from his head, I would have run.*

Tiara began to reminisce. Sweat dripped down her forehead as her body temperature began to rise. The toxic mixture she had consumed was taking affect. Her hands were too heavy and tingling to wipe her head. She could only breathe, faster and faster to catch up to the speed of her racing heart. *Why did I accept that ride, those sneakers, that necklace?* She continued her list of regrets. *I should've said no. No to the dresses, the money, the weed. No, no, no to the request to teach me a few things, no to his kisses, no to his motion of pain disguised as pleasure, and hell no to sharing me with a friend.*

The pounding on the door revisited her. Too tired to care and too numb to sob, her tears just fell. With every pound, she flashed back to each slap and punch she had received, then how he had passionately kissed her bloody, bruised lips. All the times he had forced her to give herself. Her first politician, teacher, homies fresh out of jail, and now a pastor. Pastor Douglas.

Oh God, I wish I could go back and have a chance at life. Another chance to say no, A chance to walk away, someone to run to for protection. A chance to be loved.

She dropped her head into her chest. A piercing ringing sound erupted in her ears. The kitchen door burst open, but her eyelids were too weighted to open. She could vaguely feel the heavy footsteps rushing toward her. Her lifeless body was lifted off the floor. Blackness smothered her consciousness.

Detective Charles Lee approached the seemingly condemned two-family house. He banged on the front door and waited for a response before banging again. Driven by the tone of concern in his friend Adrian's voice, he slowly walked to the back of the house. He carefully maneuvered through the high weeds that grew from the cracked cement of the driveway, kicking broken beer bottles and dodging syringe needles along the way. He felt uneasy, for the deeper he went to the back of the house, the more dangerous and suspect the conditions were. He approached the back kitchen window, which was open. He looked in and saw Tiara sitting on the floor, unconscious.

He radioed in for emergency assistance then rushed to the back door and pounded. "Police. Tiara, can you hear me?" No response. He kicked in the back door and ran to Tiara's side. He felt for her pulse, which was faint. He scooped Tiara's limp body into his arms and placed her on the carpet in the living room. "Tiara? Tiara, can you hear me?" He lifted her eyelids, which revealed her eyes rolled back. He scanned the kitchen for evidence of what could have caused Tiara's body to react in such a way. Through the shattered dishes, trash, and clothes on the food-stained kitchen floor, he noticed the whiskey and pill bottles where he had found her.

Detective Lee opened the front door to allow air into the stifling hot apartment. He rushed to his car and grabbed the Narcan kit. Out of the corner of his eye, he spotted a black car with tinted windows. The driver's side window was cracked mid-way, and a caramel-skinned man with dreaded hair and sunglass sat in the driver's seat. Detective Lee was suspicious, as the man appeared to be watching the house, but the sunglasses disguised his intentions. Lee took a mental note of the man's license plate and ran back into the house. He knelt beside Tiara and called out to her. With no response, he tilted her head back and sprayed the overdose reversal nasal spray into each nostril. No response. No response.

Sirens rang closer and louder. Detective Lee ran outside to direct the EMT into the front door. "It looks like an apparent overdose. I administered Narcan with no response," he explained to the EMT. He stepped outside while they worked on Tiara.

Everyone cheered and took pictures as little Willie blew out his birthday candles. Adrian lifted his phone and huddled in with his family for a selfie with the birthday boy with the icing-covered smile. "Cheese!" they sung.

Ring, ring. A call interrupted the caption. "It's Chuck." Adrian looked at Wilhelmina nervously. "Hey, Chuck, whatchu find out?"

"A, I'm not sure right now, but it looks like an OD. Meet us at Down City Hospital." Adrian disconnected and walked over to Shy, who sucked her teeth and looked at Adrian.

"What? Why are you bothering me, Adrian?" She rolled her eyes.

"Tiara is in the hospital." He stared at Shy.

"What? Let's go." Wilhelmina volunteered to stay behind as Adrian and Shy rushed to the hospital. It was a very long and quiet ride. Tension was thick as the two steamed with anger toward each other and anxiousness toward the status of Tiara. Shy stared out the passenger side window. She couldn't take it any longer.

"What is your problem with me? Seriously, why are you so concerned with who I date, to the point where you're mad at me, Adrian? Really!" She turned in her seat, demanding answers and an end to the friction between the two of them.

Adrian glanced in her direction and snickered. She fueled his disgust toward her. He shook his head. "I…I…I don't care who you date." He kept his eyes on the road. He tried to compose himself from letting it all out. Besides, this was his wife's best friend.

"That's it?" Shy asked, prepared to have an argument.

"Look, I don't care. Honestly, I'm short with you because I have a low tolerance for dumbness."

"Excuse me?" Shy was offended. "So you're calling me dumb?"

"No. I said dumbness," he explained further. "Your choice in men is dumb, then you dumb yourself down and act like you don't know or don't want to know what they are into, which is always some dumbness that endangers you, my family, and others—which in this case is Tiara."

Silence filled the car once again. Shy had no choice but to sit in the truth that was placed in front of her. There was no way to escape the reality of her life's choices and their effects on those she loved.

The EMT placed Tiara's lifeless body on the gurney and wheeled her into the ambulance, then drove off with sirens blaring. Mike sat across the street in his black-tinted car, two houses before Tiara's. He was fuming, wishing he had gotten to her first. He wished he was the reason she needed an ambulance. He punched the steering wheel. Officer Lee was closing up the house when the faint sound of a horn caught his attention. "Shit!" Mike mumbled, not realizing his frustration brought attention to himself. Detective Lee was convinced there was something up with this guy. He walked over to the car, his hand gripping his holster, not knowing that Mike too was gripping his own.

"Excuse me, sir. Can you roll your window down, please?" Detective Lee demanded before getting too close to the vehicle. Mike slowly rolled down the window.

"Is there a problem, officer?" He turned on his "Mr. nice guy" tone.

"License and registration, please."

"Is there a problem?" Mike hesitated.

"No problem. I noticed you've been parked her with your car running for about an hour now. This isn't the address on your license." He reviewed Mike's papers. "Do you know someone in this house, or perhaps that house?" Detective Lee pointed to the house where he found Tiara's innocent body.

Mike tensed up. "I don't know anyone in that house. I saw them bring that girl out. Hope she's ok." He tried to keep a straight face. "I'm meeting my boy at his house. Right here. He should be here any moment, officer." Detective Lee walked back to his car to run Mike's information, hoping there was something he could arrest him on. There was just something about him. Nothing. Mike was clean.

"I see you were just released. Stay out of trouble." he said as he handed Mike his papers.

"I will do that, officer. You have a good day." Mike rolled up his tinted window and watched Officer Lee walk back to his vehicle. Unable to act on his suspicions, Officer Lee turned on his sirens and headed for the hospital.

Adrian and Shy waited in the emergency room for the ambulance to arrive. Shy paced the floor, refusing to sit beside a man who despised her. Adrian watched her and began to feel bad. He didn't regret his truth, but he started to regret his delivery of his truth. He walked over to Shy as she finally rested against a window across the room. She folded her arms, preparing for more hurtful reality. He leaned against the window, not sure what to say, seeing how guarded she was. "Shy," he said, facing her.

"Wait, Adrian." She lifted her hand, stopping his words. "I need to say something." She took a deep breath. "It hurts that you see me as some dumb chick. I'm a woman, Adrian. I love hard and want to be loved. I realize I have made a lot of bad choices in men. I know that, and I hate that." She wiped the tears before they could fall. "I just, I don't know. I see the way people look at me. I hear the things they say because I'm single and dating. They just expect you to get married at first sight. I don't know why I'm so interested in men who need saving. It's like they give me balance. I have to be so perfect at work and church, but a bad boy don't care. They love my flaws. Sad, I know, but…"

"Adrian!" Detective Lee interrupted.

"Chuck. What happened?"

"The ambulance just arrived. I got to the house and found Tiara unresponsive. It looks like she took pills. Do either of you know how I can reach her mom?"

Shy rolled her eyes. "Good luck with that one. She's a piece of work." She stepped away to answer her phone.

"So what made you send me to her house in the first place?" Officer Lee asked. Adrian explained the confrontation that had occurred at the house. "What does this guy look like?" Adrian described Mike's features and stature. "Does he drive a black car?" Officer Lee asked. Adrian confirmed. "Alright, give me a second." Realizing his suspicions were valid, he grabbed his phone and called his superior for advice. A BOLO was placed for Michael Pane. He needed to be brought in for questioning.

"Where is she?" a woman demanded, stomping through the hall. She slammed her hand on the nurse's station. "Where is my daughter?"

Shy slowly walked over as the nurses tried to calm the woman down. "Ms. Oakley?" Shy hesitated, bracing herself for an abrupt response.

Rina, Tiara's mom, turned her attention to Shy. "What the hell. Why are you here? You are not her mother; I am. *I* am Tiara's mother. I want you out of here. You probably did this to her." Shy backed away, unable to prepare herself for such an outburst. Kim Oakley cut her eyes from Shy and asked the nurse to see her child.

Adrian came behind Shy. "I think we should go. Her mom is here now." Detective Lee agreed.

"Yeah, you guys should go. I need to talk with her mom." Shy didn't agree. She wanted to be there for Tiara, especially since she somehow felt responsible for her current condition. But she complied, and she and Adrian left.

Officer Lee approached Tiara's mother. "Ma'am? My name is Detective Lee. I was the one who found your daughter today. I need to speak with you before you go up to the room."

"So you're the one who kicked in my back door?" She placed her hand on her hip. "Ok, so the police department's gonna pay, right?" Taken back by her lack of concern for what happened to her only child, Officer Lee became more suspicious of her involvement. "You can talk to the police department about that. Aren't you glad I got in to help your daughter? Anyway, I need you to tell me where you were today." He continued with his questions. Tiara's mom jerked her neck back, offended by the question.

Before Ms. Oakley could lash out, she heard, "Officer Lee? Hi, I'm Jen Wills from the Department of Child Protective Services." The young lady extended her hand to greet the officer.

"Oh, hell no." Ms. Oakley yelled out. "Why is she here?" she asked, pointing in Officer Lee's face. Not waiting for a response, she headed down the hall, yelling her daughter's name. "Tiara! TT!" She pushed open every door as she rushed by. She began to run as Officer Lee gave chase. He grabbed her arm and fought to restrain her as she swung her arms, snatching herself from his grip. Two hospital security officers rushed to assist. Unable to fight the three uniforms, she fell to the floor and cried for Tiara's help—a position she had been in several nights, drunk and high on the floor, screaming for TT to help her up. This time, TT did not respond. The officers cuffed her hands and forced her to the elevators. With no more fight left, she sobbed as the doors closed.

Years of heartache, pain, loneliness, betrayal, and doing her never-good-enough best as a teen mom exploded. She realized the toxic lifestyle she lived to provide may have caused danger to her baby. *Who could have done this?* she wondered. Could it have been the man she robbed during a private party last week, her stalker ex-boyfriend, or maybe one of her many creepy admirers at the strip club?

Detective Lee met them outside, where a fellow officer was waiting to take Tiara's mother downtown for questioning. "Now Ms. Oakley, I understand your desire to see your daughter. We just have a few questions we need answered, and we'll get out of your way," he explained.

Sitting in the back seat of the patrol car, she looked up. "Please just tell me she's ok."

"The doctors are taking care of her, and I'll make sure you get an update soon." With no choice, she leaned her head back and closed her eyes. Tears representing every regret fell from her chin. She wished she had been home to protect Tiara instead of stroking the ego, and more, of a client.

Rina sat in the interrogation room, waiting for the flood of questions for which she had no good answers. The door opened, and two detectives entered the room. "Ms. Oakley?" The female detective introduced herself. "Let's just start from the beginning. Tell us about your day, morning until now."

Rina thought of the woman from protective services at the hospital. Just how much was Tiara revealing? If she told her story, would they take her baby away?

"Ma'am?" The detective pulled her back to the present.

"Firstly, let me say I'm not proud of what I do, but I do what I have to." Rina defended herself before judgement came. "My day actually started yesterday at 10:00 p.m., when I got up for work. I haven't been home since. I got the call about Tiara on my way home and went straight to the hospital." She took a sip of the warm water they had sparingly provided.

"Ok, Rina, start from last night."

"I got to work at 10:45 p.m."

"Ok, where do you work? And what about Tiara? Was she home?"

"Well, I would think she was home. I...I didn't check on her or anything. You know, with it being so late, I thought she would be sleeping." She tried to defend her careless action.

They dismissed her reasoning. "But you didn't know that for sure, right?"

"Right, I did not. So once I got to work at Queen's Dominion, I did my usual—work the pole, a few lap dances, and private rooms. My shift ended at 6:00 a.m. I went for breakfast with a few of the ladies and Jim, one of the security guards. I got a text around 6:30 from one of my clients."

"Your client? So you do work on the side?" Rina took a breath, hoping they wouldn't pick up on that part of the story, but there was no turning back. "Yes. Yes, I do. Sometimes I do side jobs, like private strip parties or just one-on-one parties."

"Hmmm, one-on-one parties, huh? That's what they call it now?" the male detective asked.

"Excuse me? That's not what it's called; it's what it is." Rina became very defensive, sensing the judgement.

"Ok, ok, please continue. So your client texted you around 6:30." The female detective tried to calm the issue before Rina shut down.

Rina rolled her eyes. "Anyway, my client texted me requesting a one-on-one at 7:00 a.m. at Regency Place. I accepted. I drove to the Regency. Met him there. I left at 8:30 a.m. I had to go to the bank when they opened at 9:00 a.m. I had an appointment for another one-on-one at 11:00 a.m., so I stayed out and got my nails done before meeting my next client at The Gates Inn."

"So, what do you do at these one-on-ones?"

"Is that necessary? I mean, what does that have to do with my whereabouts? I just told you what you needed to know."

The female detective tried to calmly explain why they needed the details. "Ma'am, we need the details of your day. There may be something that is insignificant to you but could be a key to how your daughter got in the hospital."

Rina shook her head in reluctance. "I strip and give lap dances. It's a private party with one person."

"And that's it?" The man questioned again.

"Yes, that is it," Rina stated, refusing to reveal her foul truth. "Anyway, I left The Gate Inn at 1:30. From there, I went shopping at the mall downtown and out to eat lunch at the diner on Smith Road. I was headed home to sleep when Officer Lee called my cell."

"Who is Mike?" the woman asked.

Rina shook her head. "I don't know a Mike."

Growing more frustrated, the male detective became more specific. "Michael, Mike in the black Acura. He was parked outside your house today."

"What? Who is he? I don't know any Mike or anyone who drives that car." The detectives took turns questioning Rina, trying to get her to reveal the true details of her profession, the true names of her Johns she called clients, trying to get her to break. The man pounded the table and raised his voice, aggravated with her attitude, while the female detective followed him with a soft tone and compassion. She tried to connect with Rina as a mother.

After over two hours of good-cop bad-cop role playing, they were no closer to finding who was responsible for Tiara's condition. Rina slammed her hands on the table. "Look! I have told you everything. All I want is to know what's going on with my daughter. Please call Officer Lee. He said he will call with an update," she pleaded, too tired to argue any longer. With no other questions, the detectives left the room.

The female detective entered the room again and extended her hand. "Detective Lee is on the phone."

Rina snatched the phone. "Yes, hello." Tears fell down her cheeks as she listened.

"We will bring you to the hospital," the detective insisted.

IT'S HARD TO SAY GOODBYE

IT WAS THE SATURDAY AFTER THE DEATH of Pastor Douglas. The whole city was preparing to attend the funeral of this great man, and Wilhelmina and her family headed to Pastor Douglas's large cathedral church to celebrate his life. City police lined the streets, directing and detouring traffic. News vans, reporters, and a camera crew surrounded the church. A line of people from the community formed around the church, waiting to show their final respects to this great man. What a major loss to the city of Providence. Pastor Douglas took pride in his church and congregation, serving the community by feeding the hungry, offering clothing and toy drives, providing Christmas for a family in need, and serving as the headquarters for all the city's black activist meetings and counseling.

Shy sat midway in the sanctuary. She stood up from her seat to get Wilhelmina's attention. Making eye contact, Shy waved her over, then moved her program and pocketbook from the two seats she was saving. "Hey." The two greeted with a hug and snickered at their unplanned matching attire, a mid-calf black skirt, a black blouse, and a black flat and rounded lace head covering.

"Hi, Shy," Adrian whispered.

HEM

"Hey, A," she smirked, not quite over his words the other night.

"Where's my dad?" Willie stretched her neck to look around the church. The flag-covered coffin was in the front of the church, surrounded by an array of colorful standing flowers. There were cross-, heart-, and circle-shaped sympathy flowers. News cameras made sure every angle was covered. They pointed in awe at the many city officials, dignitaries, black activists, local celebrity talents like singers, rappers, and poets, and even big-time drug dealers. They shook their heads at the spectacle this had turned out to be.

It was exactly 12:00 p.m. The choir, seated in the pulpit and covered in royal-blue-and-white robes, stood in unison, and a melodious sound filled the cathedral. A sea of bishops, pastors, priests, elders, and ministers from all denominations marched down the middle aisle. In the midst was Pastor Willard, Willie's dad. The family was next to march in. With her sons on each arm, a sobbing and fragile woman wearing a long lace white dress with her head draped in a white veil led the family. This was not just a loss for the city. Lady and Pastor Douglas had just celebrated forty-two years of marriage. Lady Douglas's husband, pastor, best friend, and life partner was gone. The untimely and unexplainable reason for his death made his departure even more intolerable. The sound of her aching heart harmonized with the choir. All eyes in the church swelled with tears.

"Please be seated," said the officiant of the service. Everyone sat in silence as the officiant read scriptures from the Old and New Testaments. Willie flipped through the twenty-page program that looked more like a photo album. There were pages filled with pictures of Pastor Douglas posing with city officials, youth groups, politicians, family, and friends, and one picture popped out among the rest. Willie nudged Shy and pointed to the picture. Shy's mouth dropped open as she saw Pastor Douglas in the prison visiting room with his arm around Mike during his last jail term.

"What the hell?" Shy whispered.

"I know, huh. Maybe he was just visiting the prison. I don't think he knows him personally," Willie concluded. The congregation applauded as a soloist sang her final tune.

"We will now have words of love and memories from friends and family. Please limit your comments to two minutes each," the officiant instructed.

The line grew with all those who wanted to honor this great man. Person after person shared their stories. One of the young ladies from the youth group took the mic and began to cry. She expressed how Pastor Douglas had been like a father to her. There was not a dry eye in the room. The usher handed the girl a tissue. She wiped her tears and tried to continue before she was interrupted.

"I have something to say," a woman standing in the rear of the church center aisle shouted. Everyone turned around to see who had created the distraction. There she stood, tall, draped in a skin-tight black mini dress, red heels, a black hat, and a veil that covered her face. Silence fell on the congregation. The sound of the woman's heels echoed as she slowly walked, swaying to the front of the church.

She grabbed the mic from the little girl. "Excuse me, ma'am. I see you are eager to honor our dear pastor. Please limit it to two minutes." The officiant tried to regain order. "Oh, don't worry, this won't be long," she snapped back. "Great man, huh? Yes, a great man. A great, great, nasty old pedophile." The entire sanctuary filled with gasps. "Oh, don't worry, he's not the only one." She dug in her big black bag and pulled out a fluffy pink leopard journal. She opened it to the last entry and read. "He pressed my face on his fat nasty thigh." First Lady Moureen Douglas began to weep.

"Oh, it's not just your man, honey. Senator Taylor, you had my daughter bent over, huh?" She turned a few pages. "Detective Jacob, you dirty dog, you and your mistress had her in your secret apartment. Oh, don't leave now, it's just getting good."

Senators, policemen, detectives, and lawyers grabbed their wives' hands and headed to the door. The officiant motioned for security to escort the lady out, but she continued to scream nasty, disturbing facts from the pink journal. Pacing the front of the sanctuary, she called out any and every name she could from the book before she was tackled and the microphone was snatched from her grip.

Adrian stood up. "Let's go," he demanded Willie and Shy.

Willie felt the truth and the hurt in the woman's story. She knew there was some truth to the stories in that pink journal. "No, A. You can go. Shy will bring me home."

"Serious? Ok." He shook his head at the drama and confusion as to why Willie had chosen to sit in, and he walked out the church.

The woman squirmed as she tried to escape the arms of the security guards. Even without a microphone, her voice roared. "It's nice to put a face to a name, Elder Jim James." She turned to the officiant and stared at him as the guards forced her down the center aisle. "Jimmy, Jimmy, Jimmy. You had my baby scream your name while you choked her. You devil." The officiant slowly backed away from the podium. Looking around at all the eyes who remained to witness, he quickly walked off the pulpit, exiting through a side door. The woman continued to jerk her body, struggling with the guards. Her hat with the attached veil fell to the floor. Shy covered her mouth. Tears began to fall. The woman walked past Shy's seat. They stared at each other until the woman couldn't any longer. "Oh, my God!" Shy screamed out, crying.

"Shy, what's wrong? Talk to me." Willie rubbed her back to calm Shy down and keep the remaining nosey eyes off of them.

"That is Tiara's mom." Shy wept as she got out of her seat and ran toward the door.

The security guards forced Rina against the outside bricks of the church. They tried to snatch the pink journal from her hands. "Help!" she screamed, holding on for dear life.

"I got her. I got her." Officer Charles Lee demanded the security guards to let her go. He was there to help detail the funeral of the year. The security guards released Rina and backed away, slowly giving her the look of death. They wanted the journal. That journal had the power to destroy the city, the power to destroy leadership from the top.

Rina collapsed in Officer Lee's arms. "Rina, are you alright? Let's go." He radioed for backup to escort them to a police car. Officer Lee felt the pressure and the death threats for Rina in the air.

Shy ran down the stairs of the church and met Rina and the officer as they walked by. "Rina." Shy didn't know what to say. Tears just fell down her face. Shy clinched her chest and shook her head. She wanted Rina to know that she really had no idea. "I'm so sorry." She braced herself for the ultimate cuss out, but Rina looked at Shy.

She knew Shy really cared for her daughter. Besides, she was like Tiara's mother when she was too high, drunk, or hanging from the pole. As mad as she was with all the perverts in the book, she was just as mad with herself. "We have to go, now. Shy, meet us downtown," Detective Lee said as he and three other officers escorted Rina away.

On the ride to the station, Rina tightly held the journal to her chest and cried, "My baby, my poor baby." Detective Lee watched her from the rearview mirror, and any thoughts of disbelief went out the window. He saw the true sorrow pouring from Rina's eyes from the events that had taken place in that journal.

"We'll get to the bottom of this, Rina. I promise." The high that had given her the strength to walk into that church was wearing off. She laid on the back seat and cried herself to sleep. Detective Lee continued to check the rearview and side mirrors. He noticed a black jeep following them about five cars behind. He took several turns to make sure, but the jeep continued to follow every turn. Detective Lee radioed the make and model of the jeep. The other escorting officers took position behind the jeep. Detective Lee pulled over and tried to get sight of the occupants of the jeep as they drove by. He made eye contact with the driver. It was the security guard from the church. "Yes, sir, we are five minutes away," he said, answering a call from his police chief. "Sir, we are going to need protection for Ms. Rina. We were being followed." He ended the call and hurried to the station.

Shy and Willie rushed through the doors of the police station. "Can you please tell Detective Lee Shyanne is here?" She asked the officer behind the counter.

It's Hard To Say Goodbye

"Have a seat." He rudely motioned to the sitting area. They sat in the foyer, waiting. The elevator opened. Officer Lee and three other officers surrounded Rina. Detective Lee pulled his gun from his holster and stepped out of the elevator. He scanned the area for those who wanted their hands on the book. Once clear, he waved for the others to escort Rina out of the elevator and into the nearest conference room.

"Can I get you something to drink?" He asked, pulling out Rina's chair.

"Yes, water. I just want this over with."

"Hold tight. I'll be back. Don't open this door for anyone." He closed and locked the door behind him. Turning the corner, her bumped into Detective James.

"Detective Lee. Excuse me. I was just coming to assist you with the interrogation."

"It's not an interrogation." Detective Lee became suspicious, as per his orders, he was the only one to take Rina's statement. "This is a secured witness. I am the only officer interviewing Ms. Rina."

Detective James stared down Detective Lee before giving a smirk. "How do you know this hoe isn't lying? You can't trust her. What kind of witness would a prostitute make? I can look at that book with you, you know, just to make sure everything is everything."

Detective Lee paused as he came to the realization that the snake in front of him could possibly be in the book. Cutting the conversation short, he said, "I'll let you know, but I think I'm all set, detective." He patted him on the shoulder and walked by.

"Shy, Willie. It's hectic in here right now. We have to keep Rina safe," Officer Lee explained. "That book can ruin some important people

"Do you really think the things in that book could be true?" Willie asked. Considering Rina's lifestyle, she wondered why the police were protecting her. "I'm just saying, the things she was blurting out seemed too farfetched—like she was exaggerating." She shook her head, disregarding the facts.

"Willie!" Shy elbowed her.

"No, it's ok. I can't get into details, but I do believe her," Detective Lee said. "Shy, can I talk to you?" He walked to the other side of the room. "So how close are you and Rina?"

"Well, we have history, as you saw at the hospital the other day. But I wouldn't say we're close."

"Ok. I haven't talked to her yet, but I'm going to have to find some place for her to go. She can't go home," he further explained.

"Oh, wow. If it's that serious, I don't know how I feel about her coming to my house." Shy became worried.

"How would you feel with staying with her at a hotel? With security, of course."

After a brief pause, Shy replied, "I think you should ask her. But I'm fine with it."

"Thank you. I'll be in touch."

It's Hard To Say Goodbye

The detective rushed off to the conference room where Rina was sitting. The fog was clearing from Rina's mind, and she began to feel every bit of hurt she had tried to smoke away that morning. The door opened, and Officer Lee placed a cup and a bottle of water in front of her.

"Are you ok? You look exhausted."

"I've been up all night. After I read the nightmares in my daughter's journal, I couldn't sleep. I wanted to burn this town down."

"I'm sure you did. Is this the only copy you have?"

"No. No, it's not." She recalled the pictures of every page she had taken with her phone.

"That's fine. Do you mind if I have the book? If we're going to pursue this and get these monsters, we need the book as evidence."

Rina hesitated, thinking of every detailed, compromising position people would read of and visualize her daughter in. But she knew her story had to be told. Maybe it would help another little girl, like she had hoped someone would have helped her when she was a little girl. Rina rubbed the pink fur on the journal then slowly slid it across the table. Together, they dissected the sexual horror stories that filled every page. Detective Lee wrote down all the names of the predators, male and female, that had violated this young teen. He cringed and grinded his teeth every time a familiar name was mentioned. Rina wiped the tears as she heard of all the people from whom she has failed to protect her daughter.

"We need to find this character 'Deuce,' Detective Lee said. "I hate to say it, but it looks like he is her pimp." Rina burst into tears. The very thing she was so proud of not having—a pimp—the very thing she did not allow herself to be—pimped—had taken her daughter.

Shy and Willie stood outside the police station, talking about the day's events. The news vans surrounded the place, waiting for any word to share with the people of the city. Any word of hope discrediting the lies that had spewed out of the mystery lady's mouth. Sirens filled the air. A notification alarm went off on Willie's phone. "Hey, there's a women's service tomorrow night. Oh, Evangelist Minnie Yves is the speaker. You know she's good."

"Oh, I have to go. I definitely need to go." Shy shook her head at the nonsense that had cluttered her life.

"Maybe your new friend, Rina, can come. If anyone needs to go, it's her."

All of a sudden, an unmarked car sped to the curb. A detective aggressively grabbed a tall man from the back of the car, who tucked his chin to his chest to prevent his face from being seen. The angered detective snatched the man's hoodie from his head, revealing his dreads and dark skin. Shy froze mid-sentence. It was Mike. The detective jerked him around, as if he purposely wanted to plaster Mike's face all over the cameras. During the struggle, the detective turned Mike's face, and Shy's eyes met his. It was as if time moved in slow motion. His facial expression went from the devil to a puppy in need of help. He hoped he could reach that soft place that Shy kept deep inside toward him. Willie, not trusting Shy and that soft place inside her, grabbed Shy and turned her attention away from Mike.

"You good?"

It's Hard To Say Goodbye

"Yeah, I'm just glad they finally got him." She shook off the soft feelings she had started to get. She wanted to save him from the uncontrollable detective. "Let's get out of here."

Shy shared with Willie Detective Lee's concerns and his request for her to stay with Rina. Willie didn't think that was a great idea.

"The hate and jealousy she has toward you…nah, not a good idea, Shy." Shy knew it would be a risk but explained how this could be an opportunity to bring Rina to Jesus. "Here you go; you keep thinking you can save these devils. Then you end up hurt or in trouble. I'm with you bringing people to Jesus. Then let's pass out tracks." Willie continued to express her disapproval for Shy's new mercy toward Rina.

Detective Lee's cell rang. "Yeah? Ok, good, I'll be right down." He hung up. "I'll be back. We'll get you some food. I'm sure you're hungry." He headed toward the door.

"How much longer? I'm ready to leave."

It had been a long, emotional night and day. "I know. Please give me a half hour, and I'll get you out of here."

He left one room and entered another across the hall. "Mr. Michael, good to see you again. We've been looking for you." He sat across from Mike. "Do you have any idea why you're here?" Mike stared past Detective Lee. He had been in rooms like this many, many times before. "You're just wanted for questioning; you're not under arrest. I need to see why your car was parked outside of someone's house the other day, remember?" Silence responded. "So are you choosing to not clear your name from all of this?" Mike took a deep breath and continued to stare.

Annoyed, Detective Lee stood up to leave. Mike turned his head away to avoid any eye contact. Stunned by what he saw on the side of Mike's neck, Detective Lee said, "Is that what they call you Deuce?" Mike turned and looked at him but again responded with silence. "Hmmmm, interesting. Are you sure you don't want to talk before I leave this room? Because I have a feeling it won't be the last time you see me." Mike waved him off. Detective Lee left the room and ran to the office of the captain, where he met his sergeant and lieutenant to brief them of the facts and the new suspect, Deuce.

With everyone in agreeance, Detective Lee and another officer entered the interrogation room, handcuffs in hand. "What am I being arrested for?" Mike asked with no resistance.

"Let's see…endangering a child, sexual misconduct with a minor, oh, and murder."

"Murder?! I didn't murder nobody, and I don't know what minor you're talking about." Mike fussed as he resisted.

"We can talk more about it if you'd like," Lee said, hoping he could get a confession.

"Get me a lawyer."

"Yeah, that's what I thought. The officer escorted Mike to the elevators. The next stop was the lower level of the station, where Mike would be processed.

LORD, DELIVER HER

SHY WAS SITTING AT HOME, ALL PACKED, when she got the call she had been waiting for. "Hi, Shy." Detective Lee gave her the location, check-in name for the few nights Shy would stay with Rina, and instructions. "Any leaving needs to be approved."

"Oh, wait a minute. I have a women's service to go to tomorrow," she demanded.

"Hmmm. Ok. I can approve that with Rina attending with you. I don't want her alone right now."

"She could use it."

"So a car will be there within an hour." An awkward silence fell on the line. "Hello? Shy, are you there?"

"Oh, sorry. Yes, I'll be ready." They disconnected.

Shy was frustrated with the feelings and thoughts that had consumed her mind. She struggled with the urge to ask about Mike, but she tamed her tongue. There was no way she could reveal that she had something to do with someone like Mike. Was he really the nightmare that had tormented Tiara's days? Was she really in love with a child molester, a pimp? It was as if she was looking for validation that her compass in men wasn't broken, as Adriane had claimed it was. Shy turned on the local news and searched online for any information linking Mike to the events that took place at Pastor Douglas's funeral. The news reporters couldn't stop talking about this mystery man hauled in the police station. They played the footage from in front of the station that she had personally witnessed earlier that day.

There Mike was, struggling to keep his face hidden, but that detective snatched his hood with vengeance and uncovered his presumed innocence. Shy paused the TV right when the camera focused on his face. *What did I miss?* She wondered, looking into his eyes. Yes, he had a rough side to him, but they didn't know that sweet, cuddly Mike that would rub Shy's feet while they watched a movie, or that BFF Mike that would listen to her talk about her day while helping take out her braids. Shy was waiting for that "ah ha" moment people talk about when they say they see things differently in hindsight. That moment never came. In hindsight, there were no clues, no signs of the portrayed monster on the television.

A hard knock at the door interrupted her confusion. She looked out of the peephole and matched the badge number stamped on the officer's badge to the number Detective Lee had given her. "I'll be right out." She gathered her things and headed out the door.

Riding alongside the officer, she shook her head. What was she doing? Why would she get herself deeper into this situation? She loved Tiara and felt a little guilty that she had not protected her better. But to now volunteer to be locked away with a hostile woman with a sinful lifestyle was taking her Christianity too far.

"Lord, why can't I just pray from afar? Well, I guess I'll be the one You use to deliver this lady."

The officer escorted Shy to her hotel room. "I'll return at 6:30 p.m. to pick you up for church." She entered the room. Rina was sitting on one of the beds, scrolling through her phone.

"Hey Rina," There was no response. Rina didn't acknowledge her. Shy had assumed the tension between them was cleared, but at this moment, the tension spewing from Rina was enough to kill. Shy put her bag down and locked herself in the bathroom. She sat on the edge of the tub, shaking her head; she regretted this decision. *Lord, how can I convince this woman who hates me to come to church?* Shy got herself together and mustered up some courage to clear the air. She began to lay out her clothes for the service: a cream long-sleeved satin blouse, a navy-blue mid-calf skirt with a safety pin keeping the side split from revealing her knee, nude stockings, and black two-inch heels with pointed toes. "Check, check, and check," she said to herself.

"What are you doing?" Rina asked Shy, sounding agitated.

"Well, I would like to go to a women's service tonight, so I'm getting my clothes out," Shy explained.

"Wait. I'm not supposed to be alone, or we are supposed to go together. So how are you going somewhere?" Hand on hip, Rina waited for the details.

Shy took a breath then sat on her bed facing Rina. "Rina, I would really like it if you would go with me."

"Please, girl, stop." Rina brushed off Shy's request and went back to a word game on her phone.

"I think we have both been through a lot these past few days, and I…"

"We?" Rina interrupted. "What do you mean 'we'? You ain't go through nothing. You are fake. Your play daughter with some play situations, but she's my real daughter with some real ass problems that you didn't know nothing about and didn't help her. So please don't come at me with that 'we' mess," Rina exploded.

Shy wanted to tell her the hell she had been through as well. But how could she tell this woman that the man she thought she loved was the prime suspect in pimping out her daughter? Rina stood up and paced the floor. "I'm sorry. I know you care for Tiara. I'm just really stressed right now. I haven't had a joint or sleep in a few days. It's all reality right now." Rina knew deep down that Shy loved Tiara. She had to love her to care for her when she wasn't around. Overcome with guilt, she tried to explain why she hadn't answered Shy's calls and texts that were begging to see Tiara or at least for an update.

"It's ok. No need to explain. How is she doing?"

"She's hanging on. Touch and go at times. Her room is on lockdown."

"I am glad she's safe and praying she pulls through this." Shy paused. She wanted to give up on the idea of going to church, but something kept nudging her. "We can pray for her together tonight at the service," she said, cringing, expecting another eruption from Rina.

"Girl, I have nothing to wear to church. Look at you, all prim and perfect over there. Everybody's gonna look at me like I'm crazy with my ripped jeans, t-shirt, and sneakers."

Lord, how do I convince her that what she's saying is wrong when I feel the same way? "I dress like this because I like to and it's what I'm comfortable going to church in, but the Bible says to come as you are," Shy tried to convince Rina while convincing herself at the same time. *Come as you are,* she thought. *Yeah, right.* "Please. I would really love it if you came," She continued.

There was a long, awkward pause before Rina replied, "Ok."

Rina scrummaged through her duffle bag and pulled out her black ripped jeans, white tank top, and black oversized off-shoulder sweater. Shy came out of the bathroom well-groomed and put together, ready to enter the house of God, ready to present a lost soul to be saved. She tried to hide the judgement on her face when she saw Rina's skin-tight black jeans with the thickness of her thighs spilling out, the six-inch red heels, and the sweater falling off her shoulder, exposing the cheetah-print tattoo splattered over her arm and shoulder. Rina looked Shy over and burst into laughter at how stiff and snooty she looked. "Damn, we look like a pair of clowns walking in this place. Is it a convention or something? I don't know if I should go, I feel way underdressed." She pulled on her sweater, trying to cover her exposed bra strap.

"No, no, you are fine. Please come."

The phone rang, and Detective Lee confirmed the escorting officer was there and would come to the door to walk them out.

HEM

They rode along, one of them more familiar with the backseat of a patrol car than the other. Rina looked over at Shy and broke the silence. "You know, I was so proud that my daughter was going to church. I figured if it's too late for me, at least she can be free." Shy turned to face her, desperate to hear more of her feelings regarding their relationship. Rina hung her head down, pretending to be admiring her finger nails, but she was wondering if God even bothered to look her way anymore. *He'll probably strike me dead for even entering His church,* she thought.

"I really love Tiara. I really do." Shy signed. "I'm just sorry I couldn't do more."

"Girl, please." Rina shook her head. "I'm the one who's sorry. A sorry mother, protector, all the stuff I should've been. I'm sorry about it all."

The car stopped. Shy hurried Rina along into the church. By the sounds pouring out of the opened doors, she knew that she was missing a good old praise break. The usher escorted them down the long blue carpet-covered aisle and to their seats. The eyes that were once closed and filled with tears from praise and worship were now opened wide and filled with judgement of the curvy body with ripped jeans that strutted down the aisle. They sat two rows behind Willie, who shrugged, as she had tried to save them a seat, but the rude usher wouldn't allow saved seats for such a packed service.

The choir sang the house down, the scriptures were read, and the offering was taken. Rina sat in her seat with her legs crossed, unphased by the joy that everyone surrounding her was feeling. She desperately wanted to feel what they were feeling, but nothing— not a spark in her heart, not a tear, not a smile. Nothing. Shy sat down, winded from cutting a step behind the exhortation by the minister of ceremony. "Are you ok?" she whispered to Rina.

"Yeah, I'm good." She was pretending to enjoy herself, somewhat regretting coming. *God doesn't care for me. My heart is too soiled for a touch from God,* she thought to herself as she held back tears just from the thought of God not loving her.

The woman of God stood at the pulpit and spilled her heart of what God had given her. She continually wiped the sweat pouring from her brow as she allowed God use her. The organist backed her up in every key as she walked up and down the aisle preaching. In her closing, she calmed her tone and stood at the edge of the altar. With her stern yet sincere voice, she explained, "God can reach you right where you are. My sister, my brother, right in that dry place, right in that place of confusion, right in that dirty, filthy, grimy place. Luke 19:10 says, 'For the Son of man is come to seek and to save that which was lost.' You may feel lost, like a ship without a sail. But God is right there. Are you ready to surrender the fight to a God that is well prepared, well armed for any battle? He's so prepared that He has already won the fight for you. You just have to take the first step to show Him that you surrender. Take that first step and come to the altar. Show God that you trust Him to handle this battle. Come, come to the altar. There's nothing too complicated, too messy, too confusing. Come."

One by one, women from every row flooded the front of the church. Willie turned in her seat and locked eyes with Shy. She motioned for her to check her phone. Shy looked down at her phone and saw a text that read: *"See if she wants to go up for prayer. That message was just for her..."*

Shy was nervous but felt she had a job to do by bringing Rina to Christ. She leaned over. "Hey, I'm going to go up. Do you want to go with me?" Shy played reverse psychology. Rina stared at her for a few seconds. She wasn't sure if she really wanted to go up in front of everyone. *Why can't God just touch me from my seat?* she wondered.

"Just come with me. There's nothing wrong with prayer, right?" Shy pressed. She stood up and grabbed Rina's hand. Rina didn't resist. She didn't know what else to do in her messy situation. Prayer definitely couldn't make it worse.

They proceeded down the aisle. Willie followed them, wanting to assist in praying for a breakthrough for Rina. They stood toward the back of the crowd. Rina's heart was racing as she witnessed women falling to the floor or jumping around. She took one step back as the preacher lady made her way to the back of the crowd. Shy grabbed Rina's hand harder. "It's ok," she whispered. The woman of God was quickly approaching. She had a serious, bold look in her eyes, like she was about business.

She locked eyes with Rina, who immediately put her head down, trying to avoid eye contact. She didn't want the woman to read just how damaged she was. She looked up, and there she was, standing right in front of her. "Give me your hands, my sister."

Rina placed her hands in the woman of God's. Tears fell down the preacher's face. She shook her head and said, "No, you need a hug." She held on to Rina so tightly. It was as if no one else was in the room, just Rina and a stranger. At first, Rina wasn't sure how to take this type of affection from someone whom she'd never met. But after a few seconds, she realized the preacher wasn't letting go, that she wasn't moving on to the next person, that she was really concerned about her. Rina felt the love of God flowing from a stranger into her. Tears fell from her eyes, then she let out the sound of her pain, beginning to weep. "Yes, baby girl, let it out." The preacher held on tighter as Rina's knees grew weak.

Willie and Shy stood behind Rina, clapping their hands and praying aloud, "Save her, Lord; touch her, Lord; deliver her, Lord."

Rina was dazed with all of the emotions that forced themselves from her body. An altar worker came and assisted her to a nearby seat as she continued to cry softly and catch her breath. Shy and Willie started to follow behind them when the woman of God said, "Wait!" pointing at Shy. "You are in need of prayer, my sister." Shy pointed to herself, confused, as she was only there as a support for Rina. She lifted her hands, and the woman of God leaned in her ear. Tears spilled from Shy's eyes. It was as if this woman was a fly on the wall in all of her relationships. She explained how God was not pleased with Shy's lifestyle and that it was time for her to completely choose. The woman of God poured oil on her hand, placed her palm over Shy's forehead, and began to pray. Shy began to rock back and forth. She started marching in place. Once the woman of God finished praying, Shy began to jump up and down and scream out, "Yes, Lord! Yes, Lord!" over and over again.

Willie wiped tears from her eyes as she assisted the altar workers with keeping Shy contained in her space. The woman of God wiped sweat from her face, took a sip of water, and began to speak in tongues as she made her way to Willie. "Broken no more! Broken no more! Broken no more!" she shouted as she tapped Willie in the center of chest with each sentence, symbolizing breaking the bond of brokenness over Willie's life. Willie fought back the tears. She thought of all the people there who knew her and her family.

What would they think if her brokenness was revealed? But the preacher wouldn't stop.

She continued..."Broken no more. Broken no more." She told Willie to say it with her. Together, they declared, "Broken no more. Broken no more. Broken no more." After that third time, Willie could no longer fight it. She stretched her hands out wide, threw back her head, and cried out. She was tired of carrying heavy burdens. The woman of God pressed on her stomach and shouted, "Broken no more!" Willie felt the Spirit of the Lord upon her. She bent over and began to speak in tongues. She fell to her knees and worshipped God. The altar workers rushed to lay tissues directly beneath Willie's face, as everything that broke her spewed from her mouth.

There they were. All three women in different positions in their personal lives, different positions in their spiritual lives, and different positions of worship, crying out to God. He didn't see the complicated mess in which Rina found herself, He didn't see Shy's conflicting lifestyle, nor did He see Willie's brokenness. He saw their hearts. He saw hearts that needed mending. Rina's ripped jeans and sexy off-shoulder shirt didn't reveal the condition of heart, and Shy and Willie's skirts weren't long enough to hide the condition of their hearts from God. He had already seen them before they entered the church. God was waiting for them to just surrender to Him and not to hem.

CPSIA information can be obtained
at www.ICGtesting.com
Printed in the USA
BVHW031353151019
561050BV00039B/273/P